A Life in Fashion

A Life in Fashion

The Wardrobe of

73 illustrations

BENJAMIN WILD
FOREWORD BY TIM WALKER

For David

Qui non dat quod amat, non accipit ille quod optat.
(He who does not give what he loves, does not receive what he desires.)

I am sorry that I cannot give more, for all that you have given to me.
I hope this is not a disappointment.

FOREWORD
Tim Walker

'Sometimes the photographs are more like the
person than the person themselves' – Cecil Beaton

I first 'met' Cecil when I was a rather lonely teenager, locked away in
a gloomy boarding school searching for kindred spirits and colour.
There he was smiling back at me from the cover of an enormous
book entitled *Beaton in Vogue*, sitting cross-legged in a candy-striped
double-breasted seersucker suit, shirt cuffs pulled out from a magenta
jumper, all under a jolly straw hat. As with all the other heavier books in
the school library, a big 'not to be removed' sticker was glued onto the
dust jacket, annoyingly obscuring some details of his outfit. To publicly linger too long on a book with a predominantly pink cover was
fodder for the bullies, so I stole the book, a forbidden bowl of sugared
almonds, by hiding it inside a copy of *The Times*, my sweaty, thieving
fingers imprinted with some important news of Mikhail Gorbachev and
Margaret Thatcher.

Back in the safety of my room I pored over the Beaton book and
the photographs I found within it: the smiling Sun King in his dazzling
picture palace with sunken ponds and free-flying parakeets; a black
and white photograph on a bridge with six friends in ribbons, ruffles
and rouge; standing with his sisters Nancy and Baba under the shade
of the ilex tree, in shorts and a cropped navy suede jacket with ten
brass buttons. Another photograph at an Ashcombe 'pique-nique', in
the same jacket, but this time in high-waisted baggy cricket slacks,
with Peter, Caroline, Bridget, Olga and King Stephen pouring tea and
laughing – all wonderful illusions of a dreamy Arcadia that my then
self couldn't possibly navigate to, stranded as I was on a forbidding
tundra of maths exams, football and foul-smelling fish on a Friday.

Last Summer some friends organized a pilgrimage to Beaton's Wiltshire. Starting at Salisbury Cathedral I remembered a story my father told me about the tiny glass box containing a fragment of the Turin shroud said to be lodged in the brass ball at the very top of the spire to protect it from lightning. After that a show at the nearby museum tracing Cecil's life, where we saw the yellow rose Greta Garbo gave him touchingly entombed in a silver Deco frame. That afternoon we climbed up to the top of the hill at the back of Reddish House still in search of Cecil's ghost. The view was so damned pretty. Picture perfect. There was the conservatory with the little jelly mould dome – surely this couldn't be the cavernous sunlit winter garden where I first encountered Beaton? An announcement was made that someone from the village had brought along an item of clothing that belonged to Cecil. We all hurried out to see a car boot being opened and a cropped navy suede jacket with just seven brass buttons unfurling onto the reddish gravel. Everyone thought the jacket was very tiny and very funny and smiled at the two-dimensional dandy lying on the driveway like a lost shadow. Cecil wasn't here anymore…he was long gone, and there were no secrets to be found. I know only too well of the fragility of the photographer's rainbow bubble and how its encircling film is liable to pop at any moment.

Another photographer told me 'It's never the same as they said it was'…and here, standing in Beaton's beloved garden, it wasn't as I'd imagined it…more of a theatrical TARDIS in reverse. Through his photographs I'd succumbed to the illusion of his world and to seek out the real thing was a mistake. Glamour is like a mirage: it evaporates as you get closer.

So then how lucky we are to have this album packed full of twinkling selfies; this is where the real Cecil Beaton can be found, and it was within some of these photographs, observed and obsessed over as a schoolboy, that I discovered a secret set of coordinates to escape the Charterhouse grey and pursue the technicolour lies of my own making.

INTRODUCTION

When he died, Cecil Beaton (1904–80) is said to have had his eternal sights fixed on the glamorous world of fashion rather than the pearly gates of heaven, for he supposedly remarked that he wanted to go to *Vogue*.[1] The comment may be apocryphal but, from the age of eighteen, when Beaton set about becoming a 'rabid aesthete', all aspects of his life – from his writing and photography to his design work, and even his circle of friends – reflected his pursuit of the beautiful and sensuous, and none more so than his wardrobe.[2]

Beaton grew up in an England still dominated by Edwardian values and vogues. At the time of his death, at the age of seventy-six, mods, punks and New Romantics were throwing caution to the wind and shocking the Establishment with their pugnacious attitude and carefully chosen apparel.[3] The elegance of Edwardian England never lost its appeal for Beaton, as his Academy Award-winning costumes for the musical *My Fair Lady* (1964) attest, but the enjoyment that he derived from buying, commissioning and wearing clothes meant that he also incorporated elements of new trends into his dress. In this respect, the style of Cecil Beaton differs from that of many other 'icons of style' and 'peacocks' – men like Georgian dandy George Bryan 'Beau' Brummell, his French counterpart Alfred, comte d'Orsay, and film actors Gary Cooper and Cary Grant – in that it was so very personal and idiosyncratic. Beaton's look incorporated styles from different cultures and historical periods; he also made use of bold

Beaton reclining in his circus-themed bedroom
(designed by friend Reginald John 'Rex' Whistler),
Ashcombe House, Wiltshire, *c.* 1934.
Photograph by George Hoyningen-Huene.

Studio portrait of Beaton, 1920s.
Photograph by Peter North.

colours, contrasting textures and subtle detailing to emphasize his slender physique. While renewed interest in Beaton's wardrobe is part of a more general contemporary appreciation of vintage styles, it is his personal engagement with fashion, and his critical understanding of it, that makes him a unique and enduring figure in the annals of style.

Contemporaries lauded and lambasted Beaton's style in equal measure; actor and playwright Noël Coward thought it exaggerated and complained that his sleeves were too tight.[4] The literary critic Cyril Connolly, with whom Beaton attended Cambridge University in the 1920s, was more appreciative of his friend's cutting-edge sartorial choices and called him 'Rip Van With It'.[5] In 1970, Beaton's wardrobe received global recognition, when he was named on The International Best-Dressed List, along with some of the most revered designers and most fashionable public figures of the time: couturiers Pierre Cardin and Hubert de Givenchy; president of Fiat, Giovanni 'Gianni' Agnelli; and fellow photographer Norman Parkinson. Unusually, however, for a man of his time, Beaton's interest in dress extended beyond his own clothes. His extensive knowledge about clothing in general distinguishes him further from other men who might be termed, by way of rebuke, 'dandys'.

In the many articles that he wrote for *Vogue* and in his own book, *The Glass of Fashion* (1954), Beaton critically compared styles from the past and present. His work in fashion culminated with his curation of the landmark exhibition 'Fashion: An Anthology by Cecil Beaton', which ran at the Victoria and Albert Museum (V&A), London, between October 1971 and January 1972. The commercial success (and curatorial flair) of this exhibition did much to establish Beaton's reputation as a critical connoisseur of historic and contemporary clothing. The acquisitions he made for the show also enabled the V&A to augment its, then relatively meagre, collection of women's historic couture. William Banks-Blaney, founder and owner of WilliamVintage, which sells historic couture and provides vintage gowns to Hollywood's glitterati, believes that this achievement secures Beaton the title of 'father of vintage clothing', because he 'made it something to be seen, collected and curated'.[6] Contemporary couturiers and tailors, from Giles Deacon to Richard James, have also incorporated elements from Beaton's personal style and photographic work into their contemporary collections, revealing that his attitude and approach to dress have a broad appeal.

If the style and sartorial savvy of Cecil Beaton are significant, they have hitherto been sidelined by writers focusing on Beaton's accomplishments as a photographer and costume designer. It was, after all, his wartime photography (made both at home and abroad) and royal portraits that first helped to secure Beaton's position among the world's most respected photographers, and his costume designs for *Gigi* and *My Fair Lady* won him Academy Awards in 1958 and 1964, respectively. Also, and perhaps surprisingly, Cecil Beaton did not write much, at least publicly, about his own clothes. In matters sartorial, his lens was generally focused on what other people wore, chiefly because he sought to maintain a facade that screened his personal struggles from those whom he admired, envied and loved. Through his professional accomplishments as a photographer, Beaton sought personal recognition from peers and patrons – those who might help to transport him to an idealized world of beauty and easy luxury and away from his own, less aristocratic, origins. At the age of nineteen, he confided to his diary, 'I don't want people to know me as I really am but as I'm trying and pretending to be.'[7]

Beaton may have been demure when describing his own dress, but his diary entries reveal his preferences and prejudices through their commentary on the cut, colour and texture of garments worn by friends and acquaintances. His observations were judicious and almost always injurious. In July 1967, an American couple – rich, elderly, loud and dull, at least in Beaton's estimation – had ruined his dinner at the Hôtel de Crillon, Paris, and provoked his ire. Recalling the incident in his diary, his remarks were bracing: 'When the two staggered out, the white slug-rat [the wife] was wearing creased pea-green trousers. What loathing crossed my face.'[8]

Even people Beaton admired could suffer his censure if he considered them to be inappropriately attired. Attending a garden party at Buckingham Palace in the summer of 1972, the year he was granted his knighthood, Beaton was disappointed by the monarch's choice of dress:

The queen, whom I respect and admire and am fascinated by,
is as dowdy as anyone....She wore a really suburban white straw hat,
a white, white coat flecked with turquoise, sensible white shoes,
a terrible glacé white handbag.[9]

Beaton was more charitable towards Queen Elizabeth The Queen Mother, of whom he became especially fond. Hosting a lunch at his London home, 8 Pelham Place, in April 1968, he recalled the arrival of her huge limousine:

Out stepped the smiling, delightful, familiar figure, dressed in
brilliant puce and magenta, the colour dazzling if the material not
of the first quality. But no complaints, everything is perfect.[10]

On the few occasions that Cecil Beaton did reflect on his own dress, he wrote with an indifference similar to that of Beau Brummell, who had recognized the absurdity of achieving fame through fashion alone.[11] Receiving news of his nomination to The International Best-Dressed List in 1970, Beaton baulked at the telegram. In his diary he confessed:

What a farce. If only people knew!
I spend comparatively little on clothes, an occasional good suit[,]
but most of my suits are made in Hong Kong or Gillingham, Dorset
or bought on quaysides during my travels abroad. I do not own
a clean pair of gloves and my shirts are mostly frayed.[12]

The thoughts Beaton chose to immortalize here are not entirely sincere. All of his comments, whether private or projected towards those by whom he had been wounded, reveal that his dress and appearance were carefully considered. He may have owned only a few good suits – although Beaton's view on what constituted a 'good' wardrobe would doubtless have differed from that of many of his contemporaries – but those that form part of the important dress collections at the V&A and The Metropolitan Museum of Art, New York, demonstrate that he possessed a keen eye for detail and a desire to craft something unique.

Indeed, for a man who spent 'comparatively little' on clothing, Beaton had accounts with a large number of London's Savile

Beaton with his designs for Noël Coward's
play *Quadrille*, at his London home,
8 Pelham Place, September 1952.

Row tailors, including Anderson & Sheppard (pp. 39, 40–41, 109), Huntsman, Sullivan & Woolley and Watson, Fagerstrom & Hughes.[13] In Dorset, near to his country home, Reddish House, in Broad Chalke, Wiltshire, he had suits made by Shephard Bros (p. 95). Shoes were made for him by John Lobb (pp. 98, 99) and Nikolaus Tuczek Ltd, hats were ordered from Herbert Johnson (p. 89) and Lock & Co., and shirts came from Excello in New York (p. 64). It was not uncommon for gentlemen of this period to frequent different tailors in the town and country, or to have trousers and jackets made in different establish-ments – it still isn't – but the range of tailors Beaton visited is curious, and suggestive of a particular interest in dress, because the house styles represented are so different. The soft, rounded silhouette of an Anderson & Sheppard suit could never be mistaken for the square silhouette of Huntsman's tailoring. The variety of tailors and requisite shops that Beaton frequented hints at the enjoyment he took from clothing, as well as his penchant for sartorial experimentation.

The importance of dress to Beaton emerges most clearly at the end of his life; his Gillingham-based tailor, Mr Melvin Stroud, was among the first to hear of his death. On the morning of 19 January 1980, he received a call from Beaton's long-serving secretary Eileen Hose to cancel an appointment that her late employer could not now attend; she added that the Palace had yet to be notified of Beaton's passing the previous night.[14]

Using unpublished archival material, surviving items of clothing and conversations with his former tailors, it is possible to learn more about the ambitions and anxieties of one of the most characterful and best-dressed personalities of the twentieth century. An examination of Beaton's dress also enables us to chart the striking transition that occurred in men's fashion after the Second World War, through the eyes and experiences of a shrewd and critical judge. As the world recovered from the ravages of war, clothing styles became brighter and bolder, as people (and particularly the young) used dress to demonstrate their rejection of the turbulent past.

In many respects it could be said that the history of Beaton's style choices follows a typical biographical arc, in that he was conspicuously experimental and provocative in his youth, rather more considered in middle age, and his wardrobe largely fixed in shape and colour by the time he reached his sixties and seventies – the story of Cecil Beaton's dress is one to which we can all, in some degree, relate.

THE TWENTIES

Young and Loud in Cambridge

Sitting inside Westminster Abbey for the Duke of Windsor's funeral in 1973, and with characteristic immodesty, Beaton informed his dear friend Lady Diana Cooper that he had 'the eyes of a lynx'.[15] Beaton's innate ability to dissect the attitudes, actions and attire of the people around him was used to great effect during his time at Cambridge University, between 1922 and 1925, where his studies were dictated by the 'university of life', rather than any College-approved syllabus. Surrounded, for the first time, by the kind of people he wanted to be like and live like, Beaton made use of his skills in photography and design, his passion for the theatre and his talents as a serial social-izer to ingratiate himself with those who could, directly or discreetly, help him to realize his aspirations of becoming an extraordinary photographer and Society stalwart. The pressure to fit in stirred inse-curities about his personal and professional status, which were to recur throughout Beaton's life, as he tried to forget his conservative upbringing and recast himself as a cultured and erudite sophisticate. In his diaries from this time, his outlook consequently vacillates between the philosophical and pompous. On publication of the first highly edited volume of these diaries in 1961, lifelong friend Christopher

Self-portrait, *c.* 1928. Beaton's style was already
lauded by friends, including aristocrat and socialite
Stephen Tennant, who had some of Beaton's suits
copied by his family tailor, Lesley & Roberts.

Beaton (far right, in a tight-waisted jacket)
with (left to right) his father Ernest, sister Nancy,
brother Reggie and mother Esther on
a family holiday, *c.* 1925.

Isherwood was struck by the artificiality and effort evinced by the young Beaton's endeavours and declared it a 'sad book'. He explained:

It's sad because you feel – at least I felt – that this whole safari
of Cecil's in search of The Real Right Set is in itself a frustration;
and throughout it, he seems so agonizingly lonely. He is an
extraordinarily heroic figure. In the last resort, he has nothing
except his work. No friends. No alleviating vices.
No real faith. Nothing. And he knows that.[16]

The rifts within Beaton's character were reflected in his wardrobe, which, during these early years, was clamorous rather than considered.

*

In Evelyn Waugh's first novel, *Decline and Fall*, published in 1928, the author fictionalized friends and acquaintances to tell the story of an imagined 'bright young thing' named Paul Pennyfeather. The photographer depicted in the book, David Lennox, was based on Cecil Beaton. Lennox's role in the novel is minor, but it seems significant that, on arriving at a party, he is shown heading to the nearest mirror to review his appearance.[17] In this fictionalization of fact, Waugh was being more than a little cruel; he had bullied Beaton when they were both pupils at Heath Mount school in London and he never seems to have accepted the young photographer's professional accomplishments and celebrity, which pre-dated his own by several years. Nonetheless, there is plenty of evidence that Beaton took great care over his look.

ABOVE
Self-portrait showing Beaton with a garter
tied around his neck, early 1920s.

LEFT
Beaton in costume, *c.* 1928. Photograph by
Curtis Moffat and Olivia Wyndham.

On 4 October 1922, when Beaton travelled to Cambridge to begin his undergraduate studies, he wore an evening jacket, red shoes, black-and-white trousers and a large cravat, eager to make a striking, and lasting, first impression.[18] Beaton's diaries reveal that the wardrobe of his youth was conceived to be deliberately provocative. Several days later, he recorded the following episode:

> I decided to buy a bright red tie, which annoyed one shop assistant.
> I said, 'is this all you have? A rotten selection.'
>
> He said, 'Well, we don't get any demand.
> No one wears a red tie nowadays.'
>
> I said, 'That's exactly why I want one.' Two other shops and
> found nothing suitable. I'll have to send to Oxford for one![19]

The look Beaton curated was certainly all his own. On a train he would wear gloves.[20] His shirts had elongated collars. His hair would be cleaned, shined and styled with a variety of products that he spent considerable time applying (so much time that his mother complained he was becoming 'very conceited' – during his youth, Beaton often clashed with his parents over matters sartorial).[21] On another occasion at Cambridge, he bought a dressing gown that he thought 'ridiculous', but he was still very pleased when a new boy at St John's College commented on it approvingly.[22] The young Beaton seems to have had a penchant for provocative loungewear. While staying in Nice in 1927, he ordered a faux leopard-skin gown that caught the eye of his dandified friend Stephen Tennant, the youngest son of a Scottish peer, and one of the most luminous of the 'bright young things'.[23] (This label, as much celebratory as it was condemnatory, was given to the sons and daughters of aristocratic and entrepreneurial pioneers, whose extensive social connections and wayward antics seemed to provide an inexhaustible supply of material for the press.) Such was Tennant's love for the garment that he bought a pink leopard-skin dressing gown on a Parisian shopping trip the following year, much to the anguish of his besotted and beleaguered admirer, poet Siegfried Sassoon.[24]

Clothes were not the only connection between Beaton and Tennant; they also shared a love of cosmetics. In his diary, Beaton explained how he enjoyed the feel of various lotions and ointments on his skin.[25] He would purchase items from Selfridges department store in London and deliver them to Tennant, who was beginning his self-imposed exile in Wilsford Manor, in Wiltshire.[26] Donning make-up was provocative, but not uncommon for the 'bright young things'. On one occasion in 1927, Beaton dined with four men at the Gargoyle Club at 69 Dean Street, London, all of whom had powder compacts.[27]

This young branch of the aristocracy, with whom Beaton very much wanted to be associated in the interwar years, revelled in their ability to shock and appal the Establishment, particularly through fancy dress. Since the mid-nineteenth century, members of the aristocracy had enjoyed a revived fashion for fancy-dress parties. The highpoint of this trend was undoubtedly the Duchess of Devonshire's costume ball, held on 2 July 1897 to commemorate Queen Victoria's Diamond Jubilee.[28] After the First World War, the desire to dress up and play

Beaton and Stephen Tennant 'duelling'
in fancy dress, Wilsford Manor, *c.* 1930s.

survived among younger aristocrats and socialites, who sought to cast aside the drudgery and deprivations of the War. Noble ancestors, historical figures and literary heroes and heroines were popular targets for impersonation. Beaton dressed as a great many real people, including King George IV (opposite), and on one occasion appeared in a harlequin costume. In 1971, for what was probably his last fancy dress event, the 'Proust Ball' hosted by Marie-Hélène de Rothschild, he appeared as the French nineteenth-century photographer Gaspard-Félix Tournachon ('Nadar'), an impersonation through which he may have intended a 'farewell gesture'. According to David Mellor, Beaton 'was impersonating the lost functions of photography in a fancy dress role of exceptionality, that of the artist-photographer.'[29]

Of course, Beaton never needed a specific event in order to don fancy apparel. In his autobiographical account of life at Ashcombe House, the Wiltshire idyll that he later rented, between 1930 and 1945, he explains:

> *The visitors to Ashcombe were often to be seen in unconventional garb. I used to encourage my guests to bring fancy dress costume in their luggage so that I could photograph them against my romantic background.*[30]

The desire to dress differently was arguably a reaction against Beaton's conventional, middle-class 'collar and tie' upbringing, and his first major foray into the world of fashion, on arrival in Cambridge, marks him out as a thrusting opportunist and social climber who desperately wanted to be noticed.[31] Throughout the 1920s, his private reflections reveal that he was envious of his affluent associates, not least

OPPOSITE
Beaton (far right) with James Ben Ali Haggin III (left)
and Mona Harrison Williams (centre) at the
Metropolitan Opera Ball, New York, April 1933.

ABOVE AND OPPOSITE
Beaton in his early twenties, *c.* 1928.
Photographs by Curtis Moffat and Olivia Wyndham.

Stephen Tennant, and disparaging of his dowdy parents.[32] The differences between Tennant and Beaton were certainly considerable; the former was well connected and well off, the latter, at least initially, was not. As the son of a peer, Tennant could be outlandish – and incur financial or social cost – in a way that Beaton simply could not.[33] Beaton's conspicuous appearance reflected an insecurity regarding the disparity between his current position and his developing aspirations. Clothing, because of the immediacy of its impact, provided a vehicle through which Beaton's ambiguous moods and motivations could be expressed.

In his private writings Beaton confessed that he was not sure why he had worn such provocative ensembles.[34] Early in the 1960s, when he started to publish his diaries (in a highly edited form), Beaton could

ABOVE
Self-portrait, *c.* 1926.

OPPOSITE
Beaton (far right) with friends (left to right)
Reginald John 'Rex' Whistler, Edith Olivier,
Zita Jungman and Stephen Tennant, southern
France, 1927.

reflect more clearly on the sartorial style of his youth. In particular, he tried to understand why he had been the subject of attention when walking through the streets of Cambridge; in a footnote he remarks:

> *Since I was probably wearing fur gauntlet gloves,*
> *a cloth of gold tie, scarlet jersey and flowing 'Oxford Bags',*
> *perhaps it is reasonable to suppose that I was noticeable.*[35]

Beaton's dress was not always outré. In part, this was because extravagant fashion required funds he did not possess. His perceived lack of money was a constant source of frustration and he fretted that 'it'll be a disaster if I'm not rich'.[36] But it is also significant that Beaton expressed periodic concerns about becoming a snob and judging his parents too harshly, both of which he wished to avoid.[37] Moderating his dress, or at least his expenditure on it, may well have been a method by which he sought to temper his adolescent aspirations; sartorial restraint as a psychological salve. He certainly believed that clothes had a transformative effect and could make him feel like a different person. Remarking on a new suit with plus fours that he received as a gift on his twenty-second birthday, he claimed he 'felt like a new person'.[38]

To make a sartorial impression when funds were lacking – or when he felt pangs of guilt – Beaton juxtaposed colours and textures, of which there is plentiful photographic evidence, if little discussion in his diaries. His appreciation of what today would be termed 'layering' and 'colour blocking' is apparent, however, in his condemnation of the dress of friends. Critiquing the new clothes of fellow student

ABOVE
Beaton in Venice, *c.* 1926. Beaton's preference
for waistcoats, which emphasized his slim figure,
and conspicuous footwear, is already apparent.

LEFT
Beaton, wearing an oversized
Fair Isle sweater and shirt, *c.* 1932.

Edward le Bas, whose grey trousers ('greyers') were poorly matched to the colour and texture of his shoes, he wrote:

> Wonderful new greyers and a double-breasted waistcoat.
> A pity about his suede shoes though.[39]

Beaton was rather more enthusiastic, in 1927, about the garb of Stephen Tennant, which consisted of plus fours and a lizard-skin belt.[40] The appreciation of contrasting colours and textures, worn in a relaxed and understated manner, was nurtured by Beaton's early travels abroad – he visited Venice in 1926, New York in 1928, Austria in 1930 and North Africa in 1931 – and by perusal of costume books, borrowed from the British Museum.[41] Beaton's early appreciation of fashion was also stimulated by his aunt Jessie, the wife of Bolivia's representative in Paris, whose stylish hats, boldly coloured clothes and 'diamond-buckled shoes' saw her throw caution and sartorial convention to the wind.[42]

The look of studied sartorial nonchalance that Beaton affected, which the Italians would have termed *sprezzatura*, became an enduring quality of his wardrobe. It is a style he adopted with renewed vigour in his later years, perhaps as much for comfort as the memories it rekindled of youthful excess and of his beloved Ashcombe.

OPPOSITE
Beaton (far left) picnicking with guests,
near Ashcombe House, Wiltshire, *c.* 1935.

THE THIRTIES & FORTIES

Celebrity and Savile Row

If the 1920s were characterized by a surfeit of aspiration over accomplishment, it was during the 1930s that Beaton began to achieve professional acknowledgment. While his career was very nearly unhinged by an uncharacteristic lack of judgment in 1938, when he was sacked from *Vogue* for including anti-Semitic remarks in one of his illustrations for the magazine – with a fallout not entirely dissimilar to that following the racist outbursts of British designer John Galliano in 2011 – Beaton's personal and professional outlook matured considerably during the 1930s and '40s, not least because of his work for the British government's Ministry of Information, whose commissions prompted him to take some of the most haunting and memorable photographs of the Second World War.[43] Beaton's style of dress reflected the developments in his life and it was probably during this period that his wardrobe went through its most marked changes. Increasingly sensitive about his appearance now that he was coming to be known on both sides of the Atlantic, the more romantic and daring clothing that had characterized his Cambridge years was now largely confined to Ashcombe, the Wiltshire home that he rented between 1930 and 1945. In public, Beaton's look was more disciplined

ABOVE AND OVERLEAF
Beaton wearing an Anderson & Sheppard,
two-piece seersucker suit for studio
photographs, *c.* 1936.

– although never demure. This was a sartorial development that owed much to his introduction to London's Savile Row in 1934.

*

Many of the clothes that Beaton had worn during his Cambridge years were characterized by a sense of frivolity and fun. This young-at-heart exuberance did not suddenly depart but, as Beaton spent an increasing part of his working life in North America and as the world of the bright young things grew dim, as the responsibilities of adulthood and the realities of work came into conflict with a leisured youthful existence, some of the more idiosyncratic elements within his wardrobe – not least the fur gauntlet gloves – were phased out.

The *fête champêtre* that Beaton hosted at Ashcombe House in the summer of 1937, when he was thirty-three, proved to be something of a send-off for his more provocative sartorial tendencies. The festivities began on 10 July and continued into the following morning. Beaton and his co-host Michael Duff cajoled guests into performing a 'Restoration manner' play, which Beaton had written with socialite David Herbert. The evening's music was composed by film producer John Sutro. The waiters' animal masks were inspired by Salvador Dalí. The guests themselves were elaborately attired, their costumes looking to Greek mythology, a fantasized Orient and Victorian England.[44] During the celebrations, Beaton wore three different outfits, the first of which was a stylized rabbit costume, whose coat (p. 44) – made of cream corduroy and decorated with pink muslin flowers, green woollen yarn (to resemble foliage), plastic eggshells and egg whites – is now in the collection of the Victoria and Albert Museum, London.[45]

OPPOSITE
Beaton in fancy dress, 1935.
Photograph by Gordon Anthony.

ABOVE
Beaton posing in his 'Rabbit' coat, 1937.
Photograph by Gordon Anthony.

OPPOSITE
'Rabbit' coat, cream corduroy decorated with pink
muslin flowers, green woollen yarn, and plastic
eggshells and egg whites, 1937. Made by Beaton.

Whimsical outfits like this, which were conceived and crafted by Beaton, reveal much about his character, but widely reproduced images of his fancy dress and made-up face have probably had a disproportionate influence in shaping attitudes towards his clothing and appearance. In fact, the majority of these garments would have been worn for only a few hours on a couple of occasions. More revealing, though on the face of it only marginally less theatrical, are the garments that Beaton ordered from Lanz of Salzburg – a purveyor of traditional costume – when he visited Austria between 1930 and 1935. Austria had become a popular destination for well-heeled Europeans during the interwar years and Alpine-style garments were much in vogue before the Second World War.[46] Just north of the Alps, Salzburg was within easy reach of two of Europe's cultural capitals: Munich and Vienna. The author Stefan Zweig, who lived in Salzburg between 1919 and 1934, described it as an 'open-minded and particularly receptive' city, which 'attracted the most disparate of forces, relaxed their tensions, eased and placated them'.[47]

Beaton bequeathed the majority of his Austrian clothes – six jackets and two waistcoats – to The Metropolitan Museum of Art in New York in 1974 (p. 49). One of his more striking commissions from Lanz, a set of military-style clothes (p. 51), he gave to the V&A in 1980. The jacket, which measures roughly 16 inches (41 cm) across the shoulders and 27½ inches (70 cm) from the nape of the neck to the waist, is of a crimson woollen cloth. The cuffs are faced with black wool and lined with green serge. Two vertical rows, of sixteen silver buttons each, were originally sewn onto the front, although only two of these remain. The accompanying trousers are of black barathea, with two

Beaton wearing a Lanz of Salzburg jacket with
zebra-print pumps in the studio at Ashcombe House,
Wiltshire, June 1934. Photograph by Sasha.

OPPOSITE
Beaton wearing a cream wool jacket from
Lanz of Salzburg at his desk in the Waldorf
Astoria, New York, January 1934.

RIGHT
Jacket (worn opposite), cream wool, *c*. 1934.
Made by Lanz of Salzburg.

BELOW
Jacket, embroidered blue linen, *c*. 1934.
Made by Lanz of Salzburg.

ABOVE
Beaton wearing a scarlet jacket from Lanz
of Salzburg in the studio at Ashcombe House,
Wiltshire, 1937.

OPPOSITE
Suit (worn above), woollen cloth lined with serge
(jacket) and black barathea (trousers), bought
c. 1935. Made by Lanz of Salzburg.

green stripes, one wider than the other, running along the outside leg. The waistcoat, the front of which is decorated with frogging and forty-four metal buttons with embossed floral designs, is of a black cloth lined with piled cotton. Colour and playfulness are ascendant in this garment, but there is also a greater degree of discipline and control than is seen in Beaton's earlier wardrobe, not least because he did not make it himself.

Another garment that illustrates the controlled creativity of Beaton's style at this time is a quilted cotton, double-breasted jacket decorated with a madder-printed floral motif (opposite). The jacket measures just over 17 inches (43 cm) across the shoulders and nearly 22 inches (56 cm) from the nape of the neck to the waist, these dimensions suggesting that it was worn as an outer garment. The jacket is lined with a blue-and-yellow checked cotton that contrasts with the madder print. Chased silver buttons decorate the collar. The precise date of the jacket's creation is unknown; the V&A's catalogue conservatively suggests that it was commissioned 'before 1977', however the style and size would make the 1930s feasible. As with the Austrian suit, colour and contrasting textures are apparent, but a certain discipline is achieved by virtue of the fact that the jacket is professionally tailored. Imaginative and unique though they are, the quality and craftsmanship that are apparent in all of these garments represent a turning point in Beaton's developing style. Combining fun and finesse, they also instantiate one of the defining features of his adult wardrobe – short jackets that emphasized his slender waist.

There were two reasons why a sartorial shift occurred in the 1930s. Firstly, Beaton's growing reputation caused him to reflect more

OPPOSITE
Double-breasted jacket, cotton, *c.* 1930s.
Maker unknown.

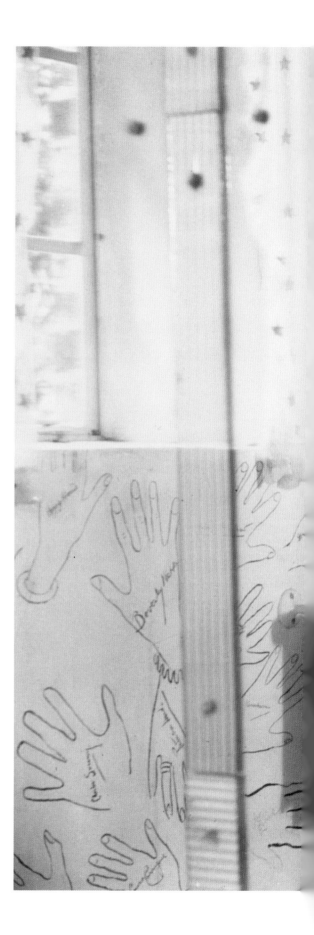

ABOVE
Self-portrait showing Beaton in Austrian garb,
Ashcombe House, Wiltshire, 1935.

RIGHT
Beaton in a Lanz of Salzburg jacket,
with the autographed 'hands' of his guests
on the bathroom walls at Ashcombe House,
Wiltshire, 1934. Photograph by Sasha.

Beaton with friends, wearing the 'scanty'
shorts he felt unable to wear in public,
Ashcombe House, Wiltshire, 1930s.

critically on how he was perceived. Diary entries reveal that bracing comments about his dress from new American acquaintances were a cause for concern. The author and playwright Beverley Nichols advised him to stop wearing make-up, a practice he vehemently, and curiously, denied in his diary.[48] Noël Coward said that Beaton wore 'conspicuously exaggerated' clothes, and with good reason.[49] During a trip to America in 1932, and for his first meeting with the glamorous actress Greta Garbo, he had worn a 'pristine white kid coat, sharkskin shorts, and new white shoes and socks'.[50] These clothes were all new purchases, along with 'football vests, exotic footgear [and] the scant-iest shorts in all colours'.[51] Excited as Beaton was with all that he had bought, his diary entry also asserts his belief that these items could be 'worn with impunity only in Hollywood or at Ashcombe'.[52]

If his growing reputation persuaded Beaton of the need to control his sartorial excess in the early 1930s, then it was his introduction to London's Savile Row that helped him to achieve it. For, despite making clothes and later designing costumes for the stage and silver screen, Beaton did not know how a suit jacket was constructed. He therefore needed his tailors to give his ideas form. According to his Gillingham tailor, Mr Melvin Stroud, Beaton would typically arrive for an appointment, having telephoned to say that he 'had an idea', with a photograph of a garment similar to the one he wanted, and would indicate the features that should be kept or discarded.[53] Sometimes he would annotate the photograph itself if more explanation were necessary. None of these photographs appear to have survived, although preliminary sketches of Beaton's rabbit coat (p. 44) give an idea of the type of design pictures he produced and show that he was

REFERENCES	NAME AND TOWN ADDRESS AND CLUB	COUNTRY ADDRESS

K.

Cecil Beaton 61 Sussex Gardens W2
(Paddington 2620.)

10/1/36 12 Rutland Court (Kens 4351)

10/1/36 1 Shepherd's Close
Lees Place Upper Brook St.

2 B. No. side pkt E Jket 17¼ X 21¾. 20¾

John Mullin
17. 10. 34

6/261

\ H 5¾. 18¾. 19½. 30½. 43½. 6¼. 8. 21½. 32¾. 10" cuff. 35. 28. 13¾. 26¾. O.B.P
\ F DR. 2 pleats. 46½. 35½. 10½. 29. 38½. 23½. 20.
straight-round. No B.B. S+B hip reversed - straight-

REFERENCES	NAME AND TOWN ADDRESS AND CLUB	COUNTRY ADDRESS

NK. C

Coventry Court Hotel.

Giuseppe Bellini
c/o Marquis Cappelli
5 Dover St
London

Marquis G. Cappelli
18. 10. 1934

B.

O.B.P

Eugenio Erchin 3 France

6/259 \ B. 4½. 18. 18. 19. 29½. 4½. 6½. 9. 21. 31½. &L. 38. 32. 14½. 26. 20¾.
\ G. 44¾. 32½. 31½. 40¾. 25. 20. 2 Hips. 2 Pleats. S.B.L. cross over band.

Beaton's measurements, as recorded by
Savile Row tailors Anderson & Sheppard on
his first visit to their shop, 17 October 1934. *Vogue*
writer Johnnie McMullin's name appears at the
top of the 'References' column.

concerned with the final look of a garment, but did not necessarily consider how this was to be achieved.

It was on 17 October 1934 that Johnnie McMullin, a writer for British *Vogue*, introduced Beaton to Savile Row's Anderson & Sheppard.[54] Suits had been made for Beaton prior to this auspicious engagement, and it was common for him to receive clothes and dress accessories from family members for his birthday and for Christmas.[55] He was already something of a style exemplar; in November 1929, Beaton was informed by Stephen Tennant that he had had some of his suits copied, presumably by his family's Savile Row tailor, Lesley & Roberts.[56] However, it is unlikely that Beaton, still only thirty, had the independent means to indulge his sartorial predilections much before this point and it is very doubtful that his father, who was apparently pleased to have bought a hat in Norwich for 4s 9d (which Beaton considered 'absurd' and 'offensive') would have footed the bill.[57] Beaton's first visit to Anderson & Sheppard was therefore something of a rite of passage.

According to the measurements that Anderson & Sheppard took (opposite), the thirty-year-old Beaton's waist measured 29 inches (74 cm). His chest measured approximately 32 inches (81 cm). These enviable proportions explain Beaton's striking silhouette in early photographs. Height is another conspicuous feature of these images; he was a little over six feet tall. According to the Anderson & Sheppard notation, Beaton's outside leg measurement was 46½ inches (118 cm) and his inside leg 35½ inches (90 cm). Interestingly, if these measurements are compared with those taken at Beaton's Gillingham tailor, Shephard Bros, in 1965, when Beaton was sixty-one years old,

Beaton cooking in one of his Lanz of Salzburg
jackets, Ashcombe House, Wiltshire, July 1936.
Photograph by Sasha.

it is apparent that his trousers had been more generously cut when he was younger, which would have only made his waist seem even tinier. Comparison between the measurements taken by the two tailoring firms also reveals that Beaton retained his figure; at the age of sixty-seven, his chest measured 40 inches (102 cm) and his waist 36½ inches (93 cm). Photographs show that he continued to wear his Austrian clothing, for example, in his later years and surviving garments reveal no signs of alteration.

Emphasizing his physical attributes was key to Beaton's aesthetic and, as he grew older (and with the assistance of his tailors), he learned how to take full advantage of his slender figure. His suits were always tight-fitting; his rabbit suit measures just 17 inches (43 cm) across the shoulders, and suits for daywear, worn for much longer periods, had similar proportions.[58] To show off his tiny waist, photographs reveal that Beaton had a preference for short jackets, as his Austrian clothing and floral-print jacket at the V&A, discussed above, indicate. He also favoured three-piece suits with double-breasted waistcoats, which revealed his slender figure to its best advantage (p. 110). Mr Melvin Stroud at Shephard Bros can recall one particular commission through which Beaton seems to have tried to emphasize both his waist and height. Apparently, he wanted an overcoat that resembled a morning coat. A morning coat is not meant to fasten at the front but, for this hybrid, Beaton wanted the buttons to function as they would on a double-breasted jacket. The effect would presumably have been similar to an eighteenth-century frock coat.[59] This coat is not known to survive, but the look Beaton was pursuing can be appreciated by studying a black mohair evening suit, now in the V&A, which probably

Beaton in his circus-themed bedroom, Ashcombe
House, Wiltshire, June 1934. The murals were
painted by friends including Lord Berners, Mona
Harrison Williams, Pavel Tchelitchew
and Reginald John 'Rex' Whistler.

Evening shirt, cotton, 1960s.
Made by Excello, New York.

dates from the mid-1960s (p. 119). The suit's single-breasted jacket is cut away under the front buttons to mimic an eighteenth-century -style coat and to emphasize the waist and corresponding black silk waistcoat worn underneath.

If Beaton's jackets were worn short, to delineate the waist, his jacket collars were generally enlarged and his shirt collars were deep. A surviving dress shirt, made for Beaton in the 1960s by the New York-based firm Excello, has points of 3½ inches (9 cm, opposite). While older contemporaries such as actors Cary Grant and Walter John 'Jack' Buchanan wore modified collars to camouflage long necks, this does not seem to have been the case for Beaton – the collars of his suit jackets were never modified.[60] He apparently liked the extra shirt collar to show over his suit and, as numerous photographs of him wearing neck scarves demonstrate, clearly enjoyed the sartorial drama that the neck could provide (p. 85). He might have appreciated a point recently made by Turnbull & Asser's head of design and product development, Dean Gomilsek-Cole, that 'the area around the neck is prime sartorial real estate.'[61] Wearing longer collars had been a sartorial signifier in Beaton's youth. In June 1928, William Gerhardie, a columnist for the weekly illustrated newspaper The Graphic, remarked that Beaton's large collars were an indication of 'originality', 'a deliberate act of stamping one's personality on the herd mind, a conscious addition of inches...imaginatively and with grace'.[62] In adulthood, and when funds were more plentiful, Beaton could request larger collars on his bespoke shirting; in his youth, photographs suggest he achieved a similar look by wearing larger-sized, possibly even second-hand, clothing (p. 35, left). Occasional references in his diary make it clear that Beaton also wore old jumpers and flannel trousers when pressed for time.[63] In 1926, when trying to complete photography assignments before Christmas – 'pandemonium' – Beaton explained that he 'hadn't a jiffy to shave or dress smartly'.[64]

Establishing a basic silhouette by the end of the 1930s did not mean that Beaton's clothing became staid. Inevitably, his experimentation with clothing proceeded at a slower pace during the war years – when staying with Lady Diana Cooper at the British Embassy in Paris in 1944, he commented on his Spartan 'everyday clothes', which consisted of 'thin shoes, a dark blue overcoat and black Homburg hat' – but Beaton was now increasingly interested in the details of his dress.[65] It is in the subtle and sophisticated cut and detailing of his clothing over the coming decades that his sartorial distinction really lies.

OPPOSITE
Beaton in frayed jumper and flannel trousers
(clothes necessary when time was scant), *c.* 1945.
Photograph by George Platt Lynes.

THE THIRTIES & FORTIES
66

THE FIFTIES & SIXTIES

Fragility and New Fashions

The years between 1950 and 1969 were probably the most successful of Beaton's career. In 1958 and 1964 he won Academy Awards for his costume design contributions to *Gigi* and *My Fair Lady* (opposite and overleaf), respectively. In 1968, he became the first living photographer to receive the honour of an exhibition dedicated to his work at the National Portrait Gallery in London. Beaton himself, entering his sixties, also appeared to move easily among a new generation of artists and designers, who helped to make London, and much of the world, 'Swing' to a more relaxed, accepting and interesting beat. However, while professional success and creative stimulus were welcome, Beaton became increasingly agitated that new attitudes and styles were desecrating England's – and his – Edwardian past. Beaton did experiment with contemporary styles, as he tried to prove to himself, as well as everybody else, that he remained current, but the visible signs of ageing, not least the thinning and whitening of his hair (which he had always cherished), meant that his outlook during this period became increasingly melancholic. Beaton was particularly upset when a haircut at Selfridges department store in January 1955 resulted in him looking like 'a semi-bald man of twice my age and size'.[66] Leaving the store, and upon being asked if he would require a taxi, his terse reply was 'No, hearse please.'[67]

*

WB.9.4

PREVIOUS
Beaton talks with Audrey Hepburn
on the set of *My Fair Lady*, 1964.

ABOVE
Actors Wilfrid Hyde-White (left), Rex Harrison
(centre) and Audrey Hepburn (far right), with
cast and crew on the set of *My Fair Lady*, 1964.
The film's costumes and set were designed by Beaton.

RIGHT
Audrey Hepburn (centre), accompanied by
Jeremy Brett (left), Rex Harrison (right) and
Wilfrid Hyde-White (far right) in the 'Ascot' scene
from *My Fair Lady*, 1964. Harrison wears a tweed
suit from Sullivan & Woolley.

Establishing a basic silhouette in the 1930s seems to have encouraged Beaton to experiment subsequently. Many of the suit jackets and overcoats that he commissioned after this period feature subtle details that would probably have passed unnoticed by the majority of people who saw them; however, their existence hints at the enjoyment Beaton experienced from the tailoring process. Examples of these details are recorded in Shephard Bros' order books, although the corresponding clothes no longer survive. Serendipitously, many of the details described – outer-breast patch pockets with narrow flaps, turned cuffs and six-buttoned waistcoats – appeared in *My Fair Lady* on the clothes designed for Rex Harrison's character, Professor Henry Higgins. In his book about the film, *Cecil Beaton's Fair Lady* (1964), Beaton describes how his own wardrobe, and the tailors and requisite shops he relied on to create it, informed Harrison's dress:

> *A call to Rex Harrison in New York. 'Hold on, old chap, while*
> *I look inside my shoes for Tuczek's address. 18 Clifford Street....*[68]
> *Hold on, while I look inside my coat to see if it has an address.'*
> *Sounds of laughter in the background. I am sending him one of*
> *my Locke [sic] hats to try on, as I want to influence him to change*
> *from the former hat, which has become too well known in*
> *every small city throughout the country.*[69]

All of the suits worn by Harrison in the film were made by Savile Row's Sullivan & Woolley, with one notable exception. In the famous scene set at Ascot Racecourse (opposite), Beaton had intended Harrison to wear a grey frock coat, akin to those of the other male characters, but he, never the easiest of actors to direct, refused. Instead, Harrison wears a brown, three-piece tweed suit. Beaton's official biographer, Hugo Vickers, has suggested that Beaton kept Harrison's original frock coat for himself and wore it on the occasion of receiving his knighthood on 9 February 1972 (p. 96), but this is unlikely.[70] While Beaton did wear a formal grey suit for the ceremony, a crucial note in his diary reveals that these clothes fitted him specifically:

> *I had for once tried on the clothes I was to wear (grey tailcoat and trousers and black silk hat) and although old they fitted…and I was right in thinking that some of the older men disapproved of my appearing so extra smart in grey whilst they were all blackbirds.*[71]

Copies of the paper patterns that were used to make Harrison's clothes for *My Fair Lady* survive and are presently to be found hanging as decoration in London restaurant Sartoria. Made in 1980, they can be identified by the initials 'M.F.L.' and the personal abbreviation 'D.J.P.', for Mr Desmond Peterson, a former owner of Sullivan & Woolley, who made them.[72] The templates reveal that Harrison was several inches shorter and wider than Beaton – too great a difference for any alteration to have been pleasing or possible. The photographic evidence reveals that the suit Beaton wore in 1972 was also a different style to those worn by the film's 'Edwardian' characters. A grey frock coat worn in the photograph overleaf, in which Beaton poses with three models from the film, probably belonged to another extra judging from the elegant fit. If Harrison did not agree with all of Beaton's sartorial decisions for *My Fair Lady*, he was generally predisposed towards his style, for it was Beaton who introduced him to his tailor Sullivan & Woolley (incorporated into Henry Poole & Co. in 1980).[73]

As Beaton aged and became physically fragile, his sartorial experimentation nevertheless continued apace. He seems to have become more determined that his clothes should keep up with contemporary trends, to help convey a youthfulness that his body could not. The results are evident in a grey, three-piece suit ordered from Sullivan, Williams & Co. (which became Sullivan & Woolley in the early 1960s) in 1952 (p. 76, left). While the silhouette and proportions of this suit are similar to others that survive from the late 1960s (p. 95, right), the red piping adorning the jacket and red stripe on the outer leg reveal something of Beaton's theatrical creativity. The endeavour to keep abreast of fashionable developments was important to Beaton. Due to the nature of his work, he felt a need to appear 'on trend' – his persistence in maintaining this facade says much about his professional dedication and personal insecurity as regards appearing professionally and socially confident among his peers – but the effort offered limited personal satisfaction. As he tried to change with the times, Beaton felt particularly aggrieved that his London tailors did not. In 1965, he lambasted Savile Row for what he perceived to be its sartorial lethargy:

It is ridiculous that they go on turning out clothes that make men look like characters from P.G. Wodehouse. I'm terribly bored with their styling – so behind the times. They really should pay attention to the mods...the barriers are down and everything goes. Savile Row has got to reorganise itself and, to coin a banal phrase, get with it.[74]

OVERLEAF
Self-portrait with actresses dressed for
the 'Ascot' scene in the Broadway production
of *My Fair Lady*, 1956.

LEFT
Three-piece suit, wool, 1952.
Made by Sullivan, Williams & Co.

BELOW
Ledger book from Savile Row tailor
Huntsman, recording Beaton's first order –
a three-piece, green worsted suit, October 1965.

It was probably during his self-imposed exile from the Row, between the spring and summer of 1965, that Beaton bought a grey, single-breasted cashmere coat from the house of Pierre Cardin in Paris.[75] This is one of two surviving overcoats that belonged to Beaton – the other, a black, woollen, six-buttoned, double-breasted coat, was made by Sullivan & Woolley in 1964.[76] This sartorial spat, however, like so many in his life, was short-lived; Beaton returned to Savile Row after only a few months. Beaton's diary reveals, perhaps, truer feelings concerning the sartorial status quo. He lamented the passing of Edwardian glamour, which was being challenged by a new generation of 'beatnik teenagers', 'peasants and roughnecks', clad in 'sandals and blue jeans'.[77] In June 1965, he chastised himself for being 'foolish enough' to buy suits from Pierre Cardin that cost twice as much as those from Savile Row.[78] Four months later, on 8 October, he bought his first suit, a green worsted three-piece, from Huntsman (see ledger opposite). It is interesting that Beaton signalled his return to Savile Row by visiting one of its more expensive tailors; his Huntsman suit cost £66 9s 8d (jacket: £38 13s 4d, waistcoat: £10 3s 4d, trousers: £17 10s). By way of comparison, a three-piece suit from Shephard Bros in Gillingham would typically cost around £60 in this period (jacket: £28–30, waistcoat: £8, trousers: £14).[79] Along London's Carnaby Street, one of the most popular addresses from which to buy fashionable clothing in the 1960s, a ready-to-wear jacket from John Stephen, by contrast, could cost between £7 and £10, and even this was not generally considered to be cheap.[80] Beaton may have been attracted by Huntsman's house style – a one-button jacket with high armhole and squared shoulder – which was perhaps as close as Savile Row then came to the pared-down and tight-fitting garments worn by the mods. The silhouette of this new acquisition would have been very different to that of his earlier Anderson & Sheppard and Shephard Bros suits.[81]

Beaton's clothing purchases in the mid-1960s were certainly curious. The fact that he would commission a rather traditional over-coat from one of his London tailors in 1964, abandon the Row at the beginning of 1965 to buy suits from Cardin, only to return and buy what may well have been his most expensive bespoke suit from Huntsman – all at a time when he was revelling in the success of *My Fair Lady*, his cinematic paean to Edwardian style – hints at a tension between wearing clothes that were comfortable and current. In part, Beaton's quandary resulted from his desire for ongoing creative stimulus. Clarissa Eden, Countess of Avon, a long-standing friend (whose husband, the former British Prime Minister Anthony Eden, also had suits from Shephard Bros), made the following observation, when interviewed for a documentary about Beaton's life in 1984:

> *He needed to absorb and know all about what was new,*
> *not so much what was fashionable, but what was new in the creative*
> *arts[,] and that gave him stimulus to carry on. It wasn't his desire to*
> *be in the swing, it was that he really needed that stimulus.*[82]

It was presumably in search of such stimulus that Beaton visited Yves Saint Laurent's Parisian couture house in the autumn of 1970. Now seventy-six, he thought 'it might be a good idea to become *au courant*' with the latest fashions.[83] In his diary, he confessed to falling under the young couturier's spell, but thought that the spirit of his designs was 'against high fashion and good style'; remarking on the atmosphere within Saint Laurent's shop, he concluded that he had 'created a Callot [Soeurs]-like atmosphere with leather, suede, felt and tinker's bells trailing a pheasants' feather. It is not for the middle-aged or the aged, but it is in itself an extraordinary creation.'[84] Two years later, he was far less impressed. At the end of another stay in Paris – he visited the Musée de l'Orangerie, saw an exhibition of Henri Fantin-Latours' work and learned of the death of the Duke of Windsor – Beaton 'went back to my old vomit with a visit to the Casino de Paris to see Yves Saint Laurent's clothes'.[85]

Beaton's contrasting sartorial decisions of this period also stemmed from personal insecurities engendered by his age. Modern styles evidently agitated him, but he incorporated them into his dress as he fought against illness and age. His endeavours convinced contemporaries and he appeared to move easily among a new generation of creative talent that included singer Mick Jagger (overleaf), artists Andy Warhol and David Hockney, and photographer David Bailey, who believed that Beaton could 'fit into any time' because he was adaptable, like a chameleon.[86] But, ironically, Beaton's relationship with these young artists seems to have increased his anxieties about his appearance, especially when their visions of him were immortalized on canvas.

Eighteen professional artists drew or painted Beaton between the late 1920s and late 1970s. The majority of their portraits were completed between 1930 and 1950, but five were undertaken in the 1960s. The artistic activity in Beaton's fifth decade suggests that there was a

OVERLEAF
Beaton (far right) with James Fox (left) and
Mick Jagger (centre) on the set of crime drama
Performance, London, November 1968.
Photograph by David Cairns.

growing compulsion on his part to find an artist who could paint the portrait he knew he had in him. It seems likely that he wanted an artist to immortalize his mature and professionally successful self in the same way that his dear friend Christian Bérard had (brilliantly) captured his youthful visage in 1938.[87] Between 1957 and 1960, Beaton sat for Francis Bacon twice. He also sat (in June 1960 and July 1961) for two portraits – never to be completed – by Augustus John, who first painted him in 1952. This sitting had produced a likeness of which Beaton became fond, although he still retouched the mouth before hanging the portrait.[88] In July 1961, he sat for Don Bachardy, partner of Christopher Isherwood, and, in June 1969, for David Hockney (overleaf), who had been commissioned to draw his portrait to accompany a feature in British *Vogue*.

While Beaton admired the work of these artists, all of the sittings, with the exception of that for Bachardy, ended badly. Bacon's portrait was destroyed, so great was Beaton's distress and his unwillingness to purchase the finished work. His reaction to the portrait, which reveals much about his sensitivity to his appearance, was bracing:

In front of me was an enormous, coloured strip-cartoon
of a completely bald, dreadfully aged – nay senile – businessman.
The face was hardly recognisable as a face for it was disintegrating
before your eyes, suffering from a severe case of elephantiasis:
a swollen mass of raw meat and fatty tissues. The nose spread in
many directions like a polyps [sic] but sagged finally over one cheek.
The mouth looked like a painful boil about to burst. He wore a very
sketchily dabbed-in suit of lavender blue. The hands were clasped and
consisted of emerald green scratches that resembled claws. The dry

painting of the body and hands was completely different from that of the wet, soggy head. The white background was thickly painted with a house painter's brush. It was dragged round the outer surfaces without any intention of cleaning up the shapes. The head and shoulders were outlined in a streaky wet slime.[89]

Bacon was understandably shaken by this reaction – at the beginning of the project, he thought this portrait could turn out to be among his best – but he assured Beaton that he need not buy the painting, as Marlborough Gallery, who represented him at this time, would almost certainly take it.[90] Augustus John's portrait of 1960 produced a similar reaction from the stupefied sitter because of its bold use of colour. Beaton derided the incomplete work, describing it as a 'large cartoon or poster'.[91] John's attempt the following year was felt to be little better and provoked further exasperation:

The canvas was the wild mess of a madman. Nothing was there. Just nothing: a weak daub of entrail-coloured brush strokes that fell wide of their mark.[92]

Equally fraught were the Hockney sittings at Reddish House, Wiltshire, despite Beaton being on home turf. The thirty-two-year-old artist, whom Beaton described as an 'unprepossessing, even eccentric, freak' on their first meeting in 1965, had impressed with his engravings titled *The Rake's Progress* (1961–63) and, over the June weekend in 1969, he drew eight sketches of Beaton in pen and ink before reverting to pencil, which apparently produced better results. This creative process

OVERLEAF
Beaton and David Hockney, Reddish House,
Wiltshire, 1969. Photograph by Peter Schlesinger.

did little, however, to reduce Beaton's anguish.[93] In his diary he questioned, 'How could he see me thus and still like me?'[94] Another guest that weekend, apparently sidelined in favour of the all-consuming drawings, was then-director of the National Portrait Gallery, Roy Strong. Strong recalled the sittings, somewhat churlishly, in his diary:

> Cecil is nothing if not vain, there was so much coming and
> going with piles of hats from which Hockney could make a choice
> for Cecil to wear. David's early attempts didn't go down well
> at all, hardly surprising for his graphic style highlighted
> every wrinkle of Cecil's face.[95]

Strong was not the only guest to remark on the fragility of Beaton's ego. In April 1961, Don Bachardy had spent several awkward days with Beaton at Reddish House, which he summarized for his partner Christopher Isherwood:

> I'm always aware of his trigger-sensitivity, which can be released by the
> slightest tainted breath. And yet he expects frank and firm opinions, and
> for one to take a stand – but it had better be the right stand....In a funny
> kind of way, Cecil's not a gentleman. He is much too self-centred to
> be really concerned with other people beyond the outward forms of
> politeness, and these keep slipping, particularly under close observation,
> and I see enormous selfishness and more than a little vulgarity in him.
> His sensitivity, if exposed to anything unrefined or unpretty, is exaggerated
> to the point of hysteria. To spend a night or two, for instance, in an
> ordinary hotel room, becomes exquisite torture for him.[96]

If Beaton's reactions to his portraits and their painters reveal an intense sensitivity about his appearance, the conspicuous presence of hats in them highlights the way in which he was attempting to find sartorial strategies to conceal, or at least deflect from, physical features he disliked.

Beaton had worn hats in his youth, though largely for theatrical effect. In the late 1950s and 1960s, his headwear was as diverse as his tailoring, although, as with his suits, he wore identical hats in different colours and materials. Beaton gifted two of his Herbert Johnson felt Homburgs – one in brown (p. 89), the other in black – to the Victoria and Albert Museum, London, in 1980.[97] The hats probably date from the early 1960s. A more informal, woven-nylon panama, also from Herbert Johnson, but dating from the 1970s, forms part of the same bequest.[98] Photographs suggest that Beaton wore this hat, and variants, when gardening and relaxing at Reddish House. More curious are the Tyrol hats that he ordered from Lock & Co. in November 1958. The hats themselves do not appear to survive, but details of the orders reveal they were made from dark green and medium green gabardine supplied by Burberry.[99] The commission is interesting in that it reveals how Beaton continued to be drawn to the styles of his youth. The Tyrol hats – presumably identical, as the order details do not specify otherwise – would have reminded him of the purchases he had made from Lanz of Salzburg twenty years earlier.

If his headwear rekindled youthful memories, the appearance of a more relaxed working wardrobe during the 1960s may well also have recalled the early years, when financial stringency had engendered sartorial creativity. Various photographs of Beaton during the 1960s

show him wearing open-necked shirts, scarves and nylon hats. It may be that the glut of photographs documenting Beaton's movie work in this decade exaggerates the extent to which his wardrobe changed during this period. After all, this bohemian attire is in stark contrast to the more formal clothing that he had adopted since the 1930s. However, considering Beaton's belief in the psychological empowerment of clothing, it is possible he adopted, or returned to, a style of dress that was familiar to him, and conspicuously different to that of his peers, in order to express his rejection of the mundane and homogenous sartorial landscape he saw around him.

ABOVE
Felt hat, 1965. Made by Herbert Johnson.

OPPOSITE
Beaton, in a more relaxed outfit, visits his
exhibition of paintings at the Lefevre Gallery,
London, 1966.

THE SEVENTIES

A Sartorial Swansong

The 1970s brought a mixture of celebration and sadness for Beaton. In 1970, his sartorial savvy and style were publicly recognized when he was named to The International Best-Dressed List. In February 1972, he was knighted by HM Queen Elizabeth II. Two years later, however, he suffered a severe stroke, which left him unable to use his right hand. It is testimony to Beaton's self-motivation and strong work ethic that he learnt to draw with his left hand, but the physical and psychological fragility that were the result of the stroke could not be easily shaken, and Beaton relied on a cane for support when walking for the rest of his life. Declining health did not diminish his interest in dress. In 1971, he curated one of the period's most important fashion exhibitions, 'Fashion: An Anthology', at the Victoria and Albert Museum (V&A), London. Donations to the show, mostly from Beaton's friends, did much to extend the Museum's, then paltry, collection of historic costume. After his stroke, Beaton continued to commission suits, although he now seems to have relied on his Gillingham tailor, Shephard Bros, with whom he had arranged an appointment on the morning of 19 January 1980. The meeting never took place, for Beaton had died the previous night.

*

If Beaton sometimes expressed chagrin at modern fashions, various photographs from his later years reveal that he endeavoured to

ABOVE
Beaton with Greta Garbo, date unknown.

PREVIOUS
Beaton outside his London home, 8 Pelham Place,
c. 1970. Photograph by Bob Thomas.

remain *au courant*. One particular photograph of Beaton and a rather dour-looking Greta Garbo (opposite) shows him in a contemporary outfit, although style signifiers from Beaton's 1930s are also clearly apparent: a short jacket to emphasize his waist and a large collar. He appears to be wearing a rather heavy-handed application of eyeliner. Beaton's decision to wear make-up, which is not explicitly remarked upon in his later diaries, was almost certainly a response to his continuing worries about ageing. In January 1971, at the age of sixty-seven, he wrote in his diary:

> *I still try to battle against all physical odds, and to try to wear clothes that are sufficiently attractive and unusual to take people's eyes off the horror they camouflage. And someone told me a day ago that I had been counted as one of the best-dressed in a 'list' compiled in the USA. But what's the point of my going over to Gillingham and ordering a new suit if it has to be worn with a cherry on the tip of my nose?* [100]

As a result of the oestrogen supplements that he was taking following a prostate operation, Beaton's upper body and face broke out in freckled spots in the late 1960s.[101] This must have been particularly galling for a man so sensitive about his appearance. In 1926, still only twenty-two years old, he had written, 'it is disturbing to see spots: they seem to me a complete "giveaway" of a person's secret immorality.'[102] One can only imagine how bitterly he must have felt his predicament forty-five years later.

As Beaton entered his eighth decade, and perhaps because of misgivings about Savile Row's traditionalism, he seems to have had fewer suits made in London and to have visited Shephard Bros in Gillingham more frequently, this tailor being close to his Wiltshire home, Reddish House. Few of Beaton's tailoring records survive, but it seems likely that he had ceased to be a customer of the London tailor Sullivan & Woolley by the late 1960s; the current vice-chairman of Henry Poole & Co., Mr Philip Parker, worked in the cutting room of Sullivan & Woolley from 1969 and does not recall Beaton as a customer. This does not necessarily mean that Beaton no longer visited, but the volume of orders that he was placing with Shephard Bros during the mid-1960s and early '70s does suggest that they were fulfilling the majority of his tailoring needs. Between November 1967 and mid-1971, Shephard Bros' order books reveal that Beaton ordered six suits, two overcoats and four pairs of trousers.[103] Newly completed orders could be delivered the nineteen miles to Reddish House directly, by Mr Stroud.[104] In Beaton's final years, and particularly after his stroke, the proximity of the house also meant that he could be accompanied on visits to Gillingham by his friend, the ballet critic Richard Buckle, or by his secretary Eileen Hose.[105]

The suits that Beaton ordered in his later years remained tight, but at least two concessions to comfort are discernible in his dress more generally. A conspicuous, if seemingly minor, detail on two identical Shephard Bros suits, now in New York (opposite), for example, is the longer back panel of the waistcoats – the 'snooker back', as his tailor described it. Whether this was included for reasons of warmth or modesty (when bending down to take photographs) is unclear. It is unlikely that stylistic considerations alone prompted the addition of this detail, as the back of the vest would be concealed, when worn,

RIGHT
Three-piece suits, wool, 1969.
Both made by Shephard Bros.

BELOW
Ledger book from Gillingham tailor
Shepard Bros, recording Beaton's order
of a single-breasted raincoat, 1971.

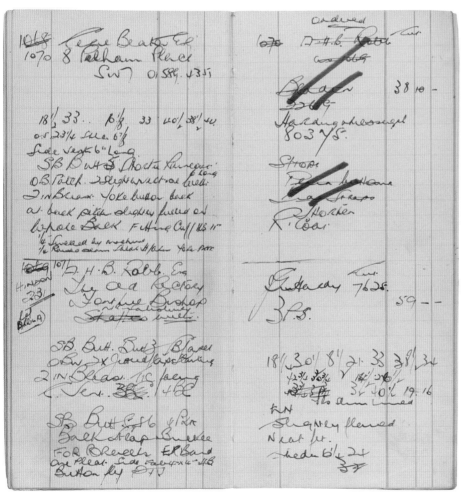

Beaton on the day of receiving his
knighthood from HM Queen Elizabeth II,
8 Pelham Place, London, 1972.

by a jacket, which contemporary photographs suggest that Beaton rarely removed.

Another preference – again, presumably, with comfort in mind – was the wearing of patent pumps. Today, this style of shoe is typically associated with evening dress, but Beaton ordered five pairs of identical pumps from John Lobb in July 1960, on a repeat order (see overleaf). Beaton had a rich social life, but it is unlikely that he would have required so many pairs for soirées alone. He certainly wore these pumps with evening dress, but photographs show that he also wore them as part of his daily wardrobe during his later years. According to Mr John Hunter Lobb, this style of shoe was relatively uncommon in England in the 1960s, but it was popular in America, which is probably where Beaton first saw them.[106]

As ever, practicality was never without panache. A distinguishing detail of Beaton's dress, which became more pronounced as he aged, was the bellow or flare on his trousers. If photographic evidence suggests that his trousers were straight or generously cut in his youth, then measurements for suits that Beaton commissioned from Shephard Bros in the 1960s and '70s show that the hem of his trousers was typically an inch (2.5 cm) wider than the measurement taken at the knee. This flare was increased in later suits. In 1971, for example, Beaton ordered two single-breasted suits from Shephard Bros, in which the very bottom of the trouser leg was belled to 18 inches (46 cm), making it at least two inches wider than the trouser at the knee; annotations in the Shephard Bros order book for this suit style refer to a previous order, so this was presumably a look that Beaton had tried before and liked.[107]

Cecil Beaton. C.B.E.

1957

Date		Description					£	s	d			
Oct.	1	To Balance		B/f			13	5	3	✓	1957	
"	2	Box Oxs Heeled & Toed.						1	6	✓		
		Sacks rept			H	14.15.9		4	6	✓	Dec. 12 Cas
Nov.	25	Box Oxs. Heeled.						16	·	✓	1958	
		Socks.			H			3	3		March 15 "
Dec.	18	1 pair Patent Pumps.			H	26095	13	13	·		14.15.9	
						29 8 0	29	8			14.12.3 13/7/58	
1958												
May.	2	1 pair Ben Brogs. Rebottomed					4	2	6	✓		
		counters						9	6	✓		
		Thro socks.						4	6	✓	June 6 Cash
		laces.							9	✓		
		Ben Norw slippers NOM Htd.			H			16	·	✓	4/6/58.	
							5	13	3	✓		
Nov	17	Black Brog n c Rebottomed					4	2	6		1959	
		Socks.			H			3	3		Jan 14 Cash
Dec	15	Box Ox Caps. Heeled.						16	0			
		Socks.						3	3		March 31 "
		Russia Ox. Heeled & Socks.			H 6 x 3			19	3		£1. 18. 6 20/1/
							6	4	3	✓		
1959												
June	5	Black Tuxedos. NOM. Rebottomed					4	4	6			
		Thro socks.			H			4	6		£4.9 0 9.7.59
Aug	28	Pan calf. Brog Ox. Heeled.						16	·		Nov 4 Cash
		Edges reset			H			4	6		£ 9 6 8/9/59
1960												
Oct.	7	1 pair patent pumps. flat bows.			H 31656		16	16	-		1961 25.11.60
											Jan 12 Cash

Beaton with Marisa Berenson, who
wears a black-sequin dinner suit by Chanel,
donated to the 'Fashion: An Anthology'
exhibition by Diana Vreeland, 1971.
Photograph by Norman Parkinson.

These final suits ordered from Shephard Bros represent the culmination of Beaton's sartorial journey. The jackets have a high, three-button fastening, to emphasize Beaton's height. The short waistcoats delineate his still modest waist, even more so with their longer back panel. The flare on his trousers reflects the style prevalent in the period, as much as his desire to celebrate his slender figure and height. The fabric chosen for the suits reveals a preference for tweed, recalling the apparel of the Duke of Windsor – who became something of a distant friend, certainly an important patron – and the hunting suits of Edward VII, another well-dressed royal and the reigning monarch when Beaton was born. The use of tweed hints at the ongoing importance of Edwardian values and vogues for Beaton. His friend Richard Buckle observed, albeit with reference to his diary-keeping:

> *Like Proust, with his rearguard action against lost time, and like Casanova, reliving his youthful conquests in the lonely impotence of old age, Beaton wanted to hoard experience.*[108]

OPPOSITE
Beaton wears casual clothing in the garden,
Reddish House, Wiltshire, 1970s.

P. 105
Beaton in the drawing room, Reddish House,
Wiltshire, 1951. Photograph by Paul Popper.
This antique Austrian waistcoat was probably
purchased in the 1930s.

THE
BEATON LOOK

Creativity and Control

Cecil Beaton's style reflected the vicissitudes of his life, but it was during the 1930s – when he was more inclined to let his professional achievements speak for him, rather than his clothing – that the basic elements of his wardrobe were established: a preference for three-piece suits; jackets, always a size too small, that emphasized the waist; and enlarged shirt collars. Bold colours, favoured in the 1920s, continued to be used in this period and remained central to Beaton's taste, but their usage became less raw and rather more refined. In dress, as in interior design, Beaton's diaries reveal a particular fondness for deep reds and green and a general dislike of white and of pale colours, unless they were enlivened by texture, as in the case of those sharkskin shorts (see p. 57); one can only speculate as to whether he would have been less severe in his criticism of the Queen's 'suburban' appearance at the Buckingham Palace garden party in 1972 (see p. 15) had she worn sharkskin or a white kid coat. Beaton also favoured the use of blocks of solid colour, as is evident in the design of the many hotel suites he was employed to decorate in New York (overleaf), which were replete with red upholstery and wallpaper. In dress, Beaton's preference for solid colours and subtle textures is shown by his suits, and by the costume designs for *Gigi* and *My Fair Lady* (pp. 69, 70, 74–75).

If colour was key to defining the look of his youth, Beaton used texture to enrich the clothes he wore from the 1930s onwards. His

international travels provided frequent inspiration, and he would study the changing landscape of new countries as he flew overhead.[109] In 1974, Beaton arrived at Shephard Bros in Gillingham, returned from a recent overseas trip, with a bag of blue cloth, the texture of which was apparently similar to sacking. From this unpromising material, Beaton asked for two pairs of trousers to be made. Mr Stroud dutifully did as the customer requested, although he cautioned Beaton that the trousers would probably last no longer than six months, due to the cloth's unsuitability.[110] The use of unusual materials had become a characteristic feature of Beaton's dress. In 1937, he ordered a double-breasted waistcoat from the tailors Anderson & Sheppard, to be made using the lining from a huntsman's coat. Beaton wore the waistcoat that same year, when he photographed the Duke of Windsor and Mrs Wallis Simpson on the day before their wedding (opposite). The use of different materials was particularly appealing and important – order books reveal that Beaton had numerous identically-cut clothes, shoes and hats.

The control and precision that characterized Cecil Beaton's public dress were less in evidence when he was at home. The dichotomy between his private and public appearance – which became more apparent during the 1930s, as his reputation and celebrity grew – was discussed in an interview for *Popular Gardening* magazine in 1972. At home, he said:

I tend to wear very shabby clothes I've had for 20 years or more –
a pair of jeans or leather trousers and a large peaked cap, which is
inclined to slip over my nose when I'm weeding. It still surprises me how
well-dressed my gardeners are. They always have on a collar and tie,
whereas I just wear an old handkerchief round my neck.[111]

Beaton escorting Frances Doble
to the wedding of Lord Herbert and
Lady Mary Hope, July 1936.

OPPOSITE
Beaton and Mona Harrison Williams on
Worth Avenue, Palm Beach, Florida, December
1936. Photograph by Bert Morgan. Mrs Harrison
Williams had been named 'The Best-Dressed
Woman in the World' in 1933.

If Beaton did reserve his more relaxed ensembles for the garden of Ashcombe, or for Reddish House, the clothing that he wore publicly in his later years was still able to cause a stir. American author Waldemar Hansen, who acted as ghostwriter for the books Beaton published between 1950 and 1958, commented that it was 'embar-assing to be seen with him' when he adopted more provocative or shabby clothing.[112]

Hansen's remarks raise a question about the extent to which Beaton's dress was conspicuously different to that of his contemporaries. The

Beaton (third from left) with (left to right)
Somerset Maugham, Graham Sutherland
and Alan Searle, probably at Villa Mauresque
in the south of France, late 1950s.

derisory comments that his dress and appearance received when he first crossed the Atlantic in the late 1920s confirms what he penned in private: his youthful self-presentation was conceived to gain attention. Beaton was far from being alone in wearing audacious dress, however, at least within the ambit of the 'bright young things'. Before his retreat from the limelight in the 1930s, socialite Stephen Tennant's wardrobe had been far more provocative than that of his older friend. Touring Italy with poet Siegfried Sassoon in the late summer of 1928, Tennant had worn a sailor's jersey, a pair of gym shorts and green eyeshadow. It was only at the behest of his travelling companion that he refrained from wearing a coral necklace.[113] For his second trip to North America in 1935, Tennant ordered a powder-blue Hussar's uniform from Nathan's, the theatrical costumier who supplied outfits for many of the fancy dress parties of this period.[114]

The fact that Beaton chose to confine his football vests and scanty shorts to his back garden or to Hollywood – situations in which he would be either alone or accepted for how he dressed – makes it clear that he would not permit his sartorial preferences to impede his professional progress. The more dramatic aspects of his creativity were reflected in his costume designs for the stage and silver screen and not, directly, in his wardrobe. There were still occasions when Beaton's idiosyncratic style shocked, however. In 1963, when he met Jack Warner, the producer of *My Fair Lady*, Beaton recalled:

> [his] *eyes popped with apparent incredulity when he first caught sight of me, but he appeared relieved when I turned out to be more or less human after all, and laughed at his jokes.*[115]

LADY CAROLINE PAGET AND CECIL BEATON IN A FILM: "THE SAILOR'S RETURN."

"THE SAILOR'S RETURN" (production pictures of which are here given) is the film which Mr. Cecil Beaton has been making at his country home, Ashcombe, with friends, neighbours, and yokels in the cast. LADY CAROLINE PAGET, eldest daughter of the Marquess of Anglesey, plays Tulip, the Sailor's wife.

LADY CAROLINE PAGET is here seen disguised in a mask.

A study of LADY CAROLINE PAGET by the lily pond.

MR. CECIL BEATON takes the part of William Targett, the sailor. The story of the film is by David Garnett.

Another view of MR. CECIL BEATON as the Sailor. Mr. Guy Branch is directing, and Mr. Vivien Braun is the camera-man.

LADY CAROLINE PAGET and the Peke. Mr. John Betjeman takes the part of a clergyman, and Mr. John Sutro is Tom.

MR. CECIL BEATON, jumpered, has some refreshment.

It is difficult to know the extent to which the toning down of his dress also reflected a desire on Beaton's part to screen his sexuality. He had romantic relationships with men and women, two of whom – Greta Garbo and aristocrat June Osborn – he proposed to, but his fondness for men or, as he more candidly put it in 1959, his 'great queer streak', suggests that these overtures were probably conceived to end loneliness and did not evidence deep love.[116] Biographer Diana Souhami, who has written about Beaton's torturous relationship with Greta Garbo, has suggested that Beaton's occasional negativity towards homosexuals was apparent rather than actual and conceived as a way to distance himself from confronting the truth about his own sexuality.[117] In 1923, at the age of nineteen, he wrote:

I adore to dance with [women] and take them to theatres
and private views and talk about dresses and plays and women,
but I'm really much more fond of men. My friendships with men
are much more wonderful than with women.[118]

The odd clothing combinations worn by Beaton and his peers during the 1920s, not least Stephen Tennant, certainly set them apart from the majority of heterosexual men, because they conveyed a love of female fashions. On occasion, from his schooldays onwards, Beaton deliberately adopted feminine styles of dress:

I acquired an abnormal interest in women's fashions.
Somehow I even managed to wear the regulation preparatory
school caps and felt hats so that they resembled those of the
ladies appearing in The Sketch *and* Play Pictorial.[119]

OPPOSITE
Self-portrait showing Beaton in a typically
eclectic ensemble, Sandwich, *c.* 1924.

Commenting on the glad rags worn by Beaton and Tennant at a party in June 1928, a journalist for *The Sphere* lauded their 'knowledge of clothes that embraces the female wardrobe, with a most definite artistic sense which their predecessors in the rough old days might envy'.[120] Inevitably, though, there were critics. Beaton's father had confined him to his bedroom for donning make-up and Tennant's biographer maintains that his preference for black-and-white co-respondent shoes (low-heeled brogue- or Oxford-style shoes, made in two contrasting colours of leather), which Beaton also favoured, would have marked him down 'in an army man's book as a bounder'.[121]

As Beaton's celebrity grew, and with the help of his tailors, he was able to create a wardrobe that harmonized professionalism and personality. The grey suit with red piping that he ordered from Sullivan, Williams & Co. in 1952 (p. 76, left) makes this point well, as does a black mohair evening suit held at the Victoria and Albert Museum, London, which most likely dates from the 1960s (opposite). This suit shows how adept Beaton had become at playing with sartorial convention. The cut of the jacket emphasizes the waist, but this was not the only detail that he requested. Turned cuffs of black silk contrast with the mohair wool used for jacket and trousers, but complement the silk-faced lapels and waistcoat of the suit. Lined with fuschia silk, which matches the back of the jacket and the waistcoat, the cuffs are diagonally cut. A V-shaped incision at the back of each cuff reveals the contrasting colours and materials used, to great effect. The silk waistcoat has six buttons covered in a contrasting, textured black fabric; they correspond to those on the jacket. On the outer edge of the trousers, and in place of the traditional band of silk, there is a thin

OPPOSITE
Evening suit, mohair with silk lining, *c.* 1965.
Maker unknown.

strip of embroidery. The hem of the trousers is cut diagonally, so that the rear hangs one inch (2.5 cm) lower than the front, to create a more elegant appearance when worn with patent-leather opera pumps. Amidst the frivolity of an evening soirée, most of these subtle details would have been hard to notice, but their cumulative effect would have been to make Beaton's outfit distinctive in a room of identically attired men, in much the same way that his grey morning coat made him stand out on receiving his knighthood in 1972. It was in this ability to add small details to his dress that Beaton's sartorial distinction lay.

In general, Beaton emphasized the cut, colour and texture of his suits. Unlike many contemporaries, he rarely accessorized. His expressive hands, so brilliantly rendered by Don Bachardy in the 1961 portrait of Beaton, were unadorned; he did not wear finger rings or bracelets. Pocket squares were not always worn, but when they were, they were almost invariably of white silk. Socks, on show when he wore pumps, were usually made of ribbed cotton in a solid colour, which either corresponded to his trousers or complemented his neckwear. Shoes were the only items of dress that, as he aged, continued to recall the exuberant clothing of Beaton's youth.

Photographic evidence suggests that co-respondent shoes – invariably black or brown with white – were worn frequently by Beaton during the 1920s, but his chosen footwear styles retained their boldness even after the rest of Beaton's raiment had been toned down; his evident delight in combining casual shoes with formal tailoring was to anticipate contemporary fashions. Beaton is photographed wearing zebra-print pumps with one of his Austrian jackets at Ashcombe House in the mid-1930s (p. 47), canvas pumps with a loose-fitting suit at Palm Beach in Florida in 1936 (p. 111); and black-and-white-striped shoes, with clashing, monochrome houndstooth socks, at Reddish House in the 1950s. A pair of traditional, black leather Oxford shoes, which Beaton ordered from John Lobb, probably in the 1960s, was made more distinctive by a subtle band of broguing across the toe and a one-inch heel.[122] Covering a lower, albeit important, part of the human anatomy, shoes have historically provided a novel means of conveying sartorial distinction, perhaps most strikingly when Louis XIV of France (r. 1643–1715) introduced red heels to his court in 1673.[123] This could be why Beaton felt confident about wearing atypical styles throughout his life.[124]

Actors like Fred Astaire, Gary Cooper and Cary Grant were lauded, both during their lifetimes and after, chiefly for their ability to conform to preconceived notions of men's style. The wardrobes of Astaire, Cooper and Grant did include personal touches, but always within the confines of a traditional English or American silhouette. Fashion writer G. Bruce Boyer refers to Astaire's 'blend of [an] urban English shape with casual American style' and Cooper's combination of the 'perfectly tailored European wardrobe with all-American, casual sportswear'.[125] Grant followed suit, although he was more assiduous in establishing a look that concealed his perceived physical shortcomings (see p. 65).[126] Unlike Beaton, however, these 'icons of style' depended very much on their physical appearance and deportment for professional success, so a certain degree of conformity to current and popular menswear trends was probably prudent. By contrast, and however much Beaton fretted over his looks, they did not bear directly on his ability to take photographs or design costumes.

It is revealing that, when Beaton met Cooper during a *Vogue* photo shoot in 1931, what impressed him most about the actor's dress was the lining of his jacket:

He was extremely smartly dressed with a brown hat to match his gloves, very elaborate with green spots in the lining.[127]

While this shows that Cooper's wardrobe had a personal flair, it also reveals the extent to which unique, sartorial detail mattered to Beaton. During the 1960s, which saw a revival of Edwardian styles among the Teddy boys and mods, Beaton's wardrobe may have appeared more typical. In his memoirs, art historian and curator Roy Strong describes a 'dark blue, very tight-chested, double-breasted [jacket] with side vents seemingly to the armpits' that was made for him by Blades of Dover Street; a 'Turnball & Asser shirt and tie in the same striped raspberry ripple fabric and a black fedora hat' completed the ensemble.[128] While Beaton's shirts and ties never corresponded so closely to his suits, the jacket Strong describes is similar to those he wore. The profusion of young 'peacocks', who aped Beaton's beloved Edwardian styles without having personal familiarity with them, may explain why photographs from the 1960s and early '70s show him in a contrasting bohemian style of dress, characterized by open-necked shirts, worn with scarves and nylon hats; he was reacting against a style adopted without appreciation.

The notion that Beaton should conform to a type of dress, be it 'English', 'European' or 'American', or appear similar to other men, was anathema to him. It is perhaps not surprising, therefore, that he singled

OPPOSITE
Beaton with his paintings, London, 1960s.
Wearing patent pumps with daywear would have
been uncommon in London in this period.

out few people whose dress he admired. In his youth, he identified individuals whose clothes he thought striking, but this was usually in order to compare their prodigious ability to spend with his inability to do so. One person who did inspire Beaton's love of clothes and costumes was his aunt Jessie (see p. 36), whose biography, *My Bolivian Aunt: A Memoir*, he had published in 1971. Beaton said that it was to her that he owed his 'first real glimpse of the world of fashion'.[129] Aunt Jessie did more than inspire a first 'glimpse' of fashion, however, for Beaton's writings reveal that he admired her innate artistry – a skill he considered few in his family to possess – and her ability to use clothing to mitigate against the vicissitudes of life.[130] Even after she had returned to England from South America, became financially impoverished and grew physically frail, her clothes were still worn with care and to great and enchanting effect.[131] This was most definitely a lesson that Beaton learned and applied himself. Aunt Jessie, perhaps more than any of the people discussed by Beaton in his memoir of fashion and society, *The Glass of Fashion*, demonstrated what most appealed to him about dress – the ability to express individuality.

A LEGACY

For champions of dandyism and vintage clothing, Cecil Beaton is frequently invoked as somebody who successfully combined clothing from different countries, periods and styles. He is that curious example of a person who becomes fashionable by defying fashions. Beaton rarely appears in recent best-dressed lists, but perhaps it is understandable that his wardrobe, which defies neat categories such as 'European', 'formal' or 'casual', is known to fewer, perhaps more ardent, style aficionados. Beaton would have liked this; during his life, he was certainly disparaged by the predictable turns of fashion's wheel. In *The Glass of Fashion*, he wrote:

> There is nothing new under the sun, and in art as in evolution,
> each new manifestation is merely the last link in a chain
> that stretches back to the beginnings of time.[132]

This was a point that Beaton had raised before, in a 1946 article for British *Vogue*. Reflecting on the relish with which many contemporary women followed fashion's trends, he wondered 'whether the woman of today stands a chance against the more statuesque grandeur of the past'.[133] In light of Beaton's enduring enthusiasm for historic styles, it is appropriate that interest in his wardrobe has been stimulated by a similar appreciation of clothing styles from the past. The renewed appreciation of vintage vogues has, in large part, been engendered by recent economic upheavals.[134]

Dandyism is especially likely to appear in those transitional ages in which democracy is not yet all-powerful and the aristocracy is only partially faltering and debased. In the confusion of such times certain men, déclassé, disgruntled, idle, but all endowed with native strength, may conceive the project of founding a new kind of aristocracy, which will be all the more difficult to destroy as it will be based on the most precious and indestructible faculties, and on the God-given gifts of which work and wealth cannot bestow.[135]

Thus Charles Baudelaire, nineteenth-century essayist and social commentator, describes the emergence of dandyism, a social and sartorial phenomenon that is most apparent during times of transition, when a political and economic malaise prevails. While it can be misleading to connect sartorial innovation too directly with social and economic developments (the repudiation of the suit during times of financial stringency is an oft-cited example)[136] the history of dress provides many examples of people changing their garments during moments of acute strife in response to a reassessment of their personal and professional roles.[137] In their study of fashions during the 1930s, Patricia Mears and G. Bruce Boyer have observed that 'in times of such crisis, various aspects of culture come to assume hyper-importance'.[138]

Since the economic crisis of 2008, social and sartorial commentators have observed that many men have changed the way they dress, either by reverting to traditional garments that convey authority and professional accomplishment – demonstrated by a renewed interest in classic tailoring and an emphasis on ascetic opulence – or they have eschewed the suit and adopted a softer and more relaxed sil-houette, with bolder colours and contrasting textures. The two styles are not strictly dichotomous and, in not a few cases, they have been combined, producing unusual and exciting contrasts – for example, the use of richly textured and brightly decorated fabrics in formal tailoring. What is clear, though, is that more men are looking to the past for sartorial inspiration. They appear to believe that by reviving the fashions of their fathers and grandfathers, they will obtain, or at least project, the confidence and certainty of the men who wore them. And so the dandy has returned, as Charles Baudelaire suggested he might.

While social changes have created circumstances in which people might look more appreciatively, and enviously, on Cecil Beaton's wardrobe, the appeal of his clothing has long been acknowledged by couturiers and designers. Giles Deacon describes Beaton as a 'phenomenal creative force', who combined 'lovely British wit and a sense of craftsmanship', two qualities that characterize Deacon's own creations.[139] Savile Row tailor Richard James's Spring/Summer 1990 collection was directly inspired by Beaton's wardrobe. One of the highlights, which paid homage to the rabbit costume of 1937 (p. 44), was a Nehru-style jacket in pink raw silk. The four-button jacket was decorated with yellow silk-organza appliqué roses and green silk embroidery. In 1992, the jacket was displayed alongside Beaton's original coat at the Opéra-Comique in Paris. The coat itself returned to Paris in 2014, when Belgian designer Dries Van Noten included it, 'as a crazy element', in an exhibition at the Musée des Art Décoratifs, which plotted a meandering pathway through the designer's creative inspiration.[140]

The survival of Beaton's wardrobe in museums on both sides of the Atlantic is a consequence of a deliberate, if ill-documented, attempt he made to preserve his style. It is possible he was inspired by those friends who had (sometimes inadvertently) gifted their clothes to the Victoria and Albert Museum, London, following his 'Fashion: An Anthology' exhibition in 1971. The decision to part with his clothing – particularly, in 1974, his Austrian clothes – may have been galling, but the stroke he suffered in the same year presumably gave his plans greater urgency. In 1976, Beaton agreed to auction his photographic archive, a decision that fashion historian Alistair O'Neill has suggested was conceived to 'secure an income and [cover] the cost of care for Beaton'.[141] That said, throughout his life, Beaton had given away clothes, most notably to his friend, the penurious painter Francis Rose.[142]

Beaton's personal wardrobe is not the sum total of his sartorial legacy, for his clothing designs and fashion photographs have provided similar inspiration to designers and artists. A portrait Beaton took showing his youngest sister Baba wearing a silver costume in 1925, 'Symphony in Silver', provided the idea for Giles Deacon's Spring/Summer 2012 collection, which featured models clad in metallic fabrics. Deacon says that he has 'always had a real fondness for the early pictures Beaton took of his siblings and friends; I love the frivolity, fantasy and the "make do and mend" nature of their production, which pre-empted the whole Andy Warhol "factory" by many decades.'[143] In this sense, Deacon considers Beaton the 'Andy Warhol before Andy Warhol'.[144]

Ulyana Sergeenko's creations for Spring/Summer 2014 appeared to reference the costumes Beaton designed for the 'Ascot' scene in *My*

Fair Lady. The beige cardigan that Rex Harrison wore as Henry Higgins in this film has also become popular. Most recently, it has featured in Matthew Vaughn's film *Kingsman* (2015). The film, which includes two references to *My Fair Lady*, also celebrates spy movies in the tradition of Ian Fleming's James Bond, and Savile Row style. Harrison's cardigan was just as popular during the 1950s and '60s. In the programme for the stage production of *My Fair Lady*, which opened at the Theatre Royal, Drury Lane, on 30 April 1958, Cox Moore included an advertisement for their 'casual cardigan-coat' – the 'Cheltenham'. Available in a 'splendid colour range' including 'Primrose', 'Martini Gold' and 'Mistletoe', they suggested the garment was a snip at £6 6s.

Were he still alive today, Cecil Beaton would doubtless approve the elision of style, the stage and the silver screen, for it was predominantly in these three areas that he lived his life in fashion.

OPPOSITE
Beaton dressed for Cambridge Footlights
theatre production *All the Vogue*, 1925.

NOTES

1. I have found no evidence for Beaton having actually said this. I am grateful to Beaton's official biographer, Hugo Vickers, for his thoughts on the subject.
2. Beaton, *Photobiography*, 1951, p. 33
3. See Elms, *The Way We Wore: A Life in Threads*, 2005
4. Beaton, *The Wandering Years: Diaries; 1922–1939*, 1961, p. 187
5. Vickers, *Cecil Beaton: The Authorised Biography*, 2002, p. 506
6. Author communication with Mr William Banks-Blaney, 19 January 2014
7. Vickers, 2002, p. xviii
8. Beaton, *Beaton in the Sixties: The Cecil Beaton Diaries As They Were Written*, 2003, p. 190
9. Beaton, *The Unexpurgated Beaton: The Cecil Beaton Diaries As They Were Written*, 2002, p. 259
10. Beaton, 2003, p. 230
11. Kelly, *Beau Brummell: The Ultimate Dandy*, 2005, p. 207
12. Beaton, 2003, p. 298
13. Sherwood, *Savile Row: The Master Tailors of British Bespoke*, 2010, p. 166
14. Author communication with Mr Melvin Stroud, 12 March 2014
15. Beaton, 2002, p. 254
16. Isherwood, *The Sixties: Diaries, Volume Two: 1960–1969*, 2010, p. 100
17. Waugh, *Decline and Fall*, 1928, p. 128
18. Beaton, 1961, p. 3
19. *Ibid.*, p. 14
20. *Ibid.*, p. 4
21. *Ibid.*, p. 15
22. *Ibid.*, pp. 4–5
23. Hoare, *Serious Pleasures: The Life of Stephen Tennant*, 1990, p. 74
24. Taylor, *Bright Young People: The Rise and Fall of a Generation, 1918–1940*, 2007, p. 215
25. Hoare, 1990, p. 86
26. *Ibid.*, p. 87
27. Taylor, 2007, pp. 205–6
28. See Murphy, *The Duchess of Devonshire's Ball*, 1984
29. David Mellor (ed.), 'Beaton's Beauties: Self-Perception, Authority and British Culture', in Mellor, *Cecil Beaton*, 1986, p. 26
30. Beaton, *Ashcombe: The Story of a Fifteen-Year Lease*, 1949, p. 32
31. Beaton, 1961, p. 56
32. *Ibid.*, pp. 53, 56, 60, 91
33. Hoare, 1990, p. 81
34. Beaton, 1961, p. 3
35. *Ibid.*, p. 12
36. *Ibid.*, p. 60
37. *Ibid.*, pp. 95, 155
38. *Ibid.*, p. 152
39. *Ibid.*, p. 9
40. *Ibid.*, p. 153
41. *Ibid.*, p. 79
42. Beaton, *My Bolivian Aunt: A Memoir*, 1971, pp. 28, 41
43. See Holborn (ed.), *Cecil Beaton: Theatre of War*, 2012
44. Beaton, 1949, pp. 64–70
45. Vickers, 2002, p. 201
46. Hoare, 1990, p. 206
47. Zweig, *The World of Yesterday*, 2009, p. 34
48. Quoted in Souhami, *Greta & Cecil*, 1994, p. 10
49. Beaton, 1961, pp. 186–87
50. *Ibid.*, p. 256
51. *Ibid.*, p. 255
52. *Ibid.*
53. Author communication with Mr Melvin Stroud, 12 March 2014
54. Anderson & Sheppard, ledger, p. 307, private collection (Anderson & Sheppard archive)
55. Beaton, 1961, pp. 60, 98, 152
56. Hoare, 1990, p. 146
57. Beaton, 1961, p. 53
58. Author communication with Mr Melvin Stroud, 19 March 2014
59. Author communication with Mr Melvin Stroud, 12 March 2014

60. Torregrossa, *Cary Grant: A Celebration of Style*, 2006, pp. 62–63
61. Ryan Thompson, 'Collars and dollars', *Financial Times: Life & Arts*, 12–13 April 2014, p. 5
62. *The Graphic*, 23 June 1928. Quoted in David Mellor, 'Beaton's Beauties…' (cited note 29), p. 26.
63. Beaton, 1961, pp. 151–52
64. *Ibid.*
65. Beaton, *Cecil Beaton: Memoirs of the '40's*, 1972, p. 34
66. Beaton, *The Restless Years: Diaries, 1955–63*, 1976, p. 2
67. *Ibid.*
68. Beaton is wrong here. Nikolaus Tuczek Ltd operated from seven London locations between 1853 and 1969: between 1904 and 1937, they had premises at 15B Clifford Street; between 1938 and 1966, they were located at 17 Clifford Street.
69. Beaton, *Cecil Beaton's Fair Lady*, 1964, p. 41
70. Vickers (ed.), *Cecil Beaton: Portraits & Profiles*, 2014, p. 83
71. Beaton, 2002, p. 230
72. Author communication with Mr Philip Parker, 15 December 2014
73. *Ibid.*
74. Sherwood, 2010, p. 166
75. V&A: T.152-1980
76. This coat is now in a private collection
77. Beaton, 2003, pp. 42, 83–84
78. *Ibid.*, p. 42
79. Author communication with Mr Melvin Stroud, 2 January 2015
80. Weight, *Mod!: A Very British Style*, 2013, pp. 134–35
81. Sherwood, 2010, p. 62
82. *The Beaton Image*, BBC documentary film, 1984
83. Beaton, 2002, p. 116
84. *Ibid.*, p. 116
85. *Ibid.*, p. 252
86. *The Beaton Image* (cited note 83)
87. Vickers, 2002, p. 100
88. *Ibid.*, p. 447
89. Beaton, 1976, pp. 105–6
90. *Ibid.*, p. 106
91. *Ibid.*, pp. 111–13
92. *Ibid.*, p. 132
93. Beaton, 2003, p. 26; *Reddish House: Broadchalke, Wiltshire*, auction catalogue (Christie, Mason & Woods Ltd., 1980), p. 104, Lot 404
94. Vickers, 2002, p. 536
95. Sykes, *Hockney: The Biography, Volume I, 1937–1975*, 2011, pp. 224–25
96. Bucknell (ed.), *The Animals: Love Letters between Christopher Isherwood and Don Bachardy*, 2013, p. 76
97. V&A: T.159–1980
98. V&A: T.161–1980
99. Author communication with Sue Simpson of Lock & Co., 8 January 2014
100. Beaton, 2002, p. 125
101. Vickers, 2002, pp. 544–45
102. Beaton, 1961, p. 103
103. Shephard Bros, order books
104. Author communication with Mr Melvin Stroud, 12 May 2014
105. Author communication with Mr Melvin Stroud, 28 May 2014
106. Author communication with Mr John Hunter Lobb, 6 January 2014
107. Shephard Bros, order books
108. Beaton, *Self Portrait With Friends: The Selected Diaries of Cecil Beaton, 1926–1974*, 1979, p. ix
109. Beaton, 1961, p. 169
110. Author communication with Mr Melvin Stroud, 12 March 2014.
111. *Popular Gardening* (26 February 1972)
112. Vickers, 2002, pp. 371–72
113. Hoare, 1990, p. 119
114. *Ibid.*, p. 205. See also Nathan, *Costumes by Nathan*, 1960
115. Beaton, 1964, p. 21
116. Souhami, 1994, pp. 218-19
117. *Ibid.*, pp. 20, 90
118. Quoted in Souhami, 1994, p. 90

119. Beaton, 1972, p. 227
120. Quoted in Hoare, 1990, p. 109
121. *Ibid.*, p. 81; Souhami, 1994, 10
122. V&A: T.157&A–1980
123. Mansel, *Dressed to Rule: Royal and Court Costume from Louis XIV to Elizabeth II*, 2005, p. 15
124. Giorgio Riello and Peter McNeil, 'A Long Walk: Shoes, People, Places', in Riello and McNeil (eds), *Shoes: A History from Sandals to Sneakers*, 2006, pp. 2–29
125. Boyer, *Fred Astaire Style*, 2004, p. 8; Boyer, *Gary Cooper: Enduring Style*, 2011, p. 172
126. Torregrossa, 2006, pp. 61–87
127. Boyer, 2011, p. 183
128. Strong, *Roy Strong: Self-Portrait as a Young Man*, 2013, p. 78
129. Beaton, *The Glass of Fashion*, 1954, p. 71
130. Beaton, 1971, pp. 21, 24
131. *Ibid.*, p. 83
132. Beaton, 1954, p. 107
133. Cecil Beaton, 'Is it the Clothes or the Woman?', in Ross (ed.), *Beaton in Vogue*, 2012, p. 157
134. Hugo Vickers, 'Cecil Beaton', in Irvin and Brewer (eds), *Artist, Rebel, Dandy: Men of Fashion*, 2013, p. 98; Ross, *The Day of the Peacock: Style for Men 1963–1973*, 2011, pp. 30–31
135. Quoted in Glenn O'Brien, 'Beau Brummell', in Irvin and Brewer (eds), 2013, p. 16
136. David Hayes, 'Mix and match of the day', *Financial Times: Life & Arts*, 23–24 February 2013, p. 5; Trevor Dolby, 'The day of the jacket is over', *GQ*, March 2013, p. 251
137. Davis, *Fashion, Culture, and Identity*, 1992, p. 133
138. Mears and Boyer (eds), *Elegance in an Age of Crisis: Fashions of the 1930s*, 2014, p. 4
139. Author communication with Mr Giles Deacon, 9 February 2015
140. Brooke McCord, 'Dries Van Noten: "Is fashion art? I don't care about that"', *Dazed*, dazeddigital.com/fashion/article/19063/1/is-fashion-art-i-dont-care-about-that (accessed September 2014)
141. Alistair O'Neill, 'Fashion Photography: Communication, criticism and curation from 1975', in Bruzzi and Church Gibson (eds), *Fashion Cultures Revisited: Theories, Explorations and Analysis*, 2013, p. 154
142. Beaton, 2002, pp. 134, 175
143. Author communication with Mr Giles Deacon, 9 February 2015
144. Katharine Zarrella, 'Giles Deacon Masquerades as Cecil Beaton', *Interview*, interviewmagazine.com/fashion/giles-deacon-london-ss12 (accessed November 2014)

BIBLIOGRAPHY

Beaton, Cecil, *Ashcombe: The Story of a Fifteen-Year Lease* (London, 1949)
Photobiography (London, 1951)
The Glass of Fashion (London, 1954)
The Wandering Years: Diaries; 1922–1939 (London, 1961)
Cecil Beaton's Fair Lady (London, 1964)
My Bolivian Aunt: A Memoir (London, 1971)
Cecil Beaton: Memoirs of the '40's (London, 1972)
The Restless Years: Diaries, 1955–63 (London, 1976)
Self Portrait With Friends: The Selected Diaries of Cecil Beaton, 1926–1974, ed. Richard Buckle (London, 1979)
The Unexpurgated Beaton: The Cecil Beaton Diaries As They Were Written, intro. by Hugo Vickers (London, 2002)
Beaton in the Sixties: The Cecil Beaton Diaries As They Were Written, intro. by Hugo Vickers (London, 2003)

Boyer, G. Bruce, *Fred Astaire Style* (New York, 2004)
Gary Cooper: Enduring Style (Brooklyn, 2011)

Bruzzi, Stella and Church Gibson, Pamela (eds), *Fashion Cultures Revisited: Theories, Explorations and Analysis*, revised edn (London and New York, 2013)

Bucknell, Katherine (ed.), *The Animals: Love Letters between Christopher Isherwood and Don Bachardy* (London, 2013)

Davis, Fred, *Fashion, Culture, and Identity* (Chicago, 1992)

Elms, Robert, *The Way We Wore: A Life in Threads* (London, 2005)

Hoare, Philip, *Serious Pleasures: The Life of Stephen Tennant* (London, 1990)
Noël Coward: A Biography (London, 1995)

Holborn, Mark (ed.), *Cecil Beaton: Theatre of War*, exh. cat. (London, 2012)

Irvin, Kate, and Brewer, Laurie Anne (eds), *Artist, Rebel, Dandy: Men of Fashion* (New Haven, 2013)

Isherwood, Christopher, *The Sixties: Diaries, Volume Two: 1960–1969*, ed. and intro. by K. Bucknell (London, 2010)

Kelly, Ian, *Beau Brummell: The Ultimate Dandy* (London, 2005)

Mansel, Philip, *Dressed to Rule: Royal and Court Costume from Louis XIV to Elizabeth II* (New Haven and London, 2005)

Mears, Patricia, and Boyer, G. Bruce (eds), *Elegance in an Age of Crisis: Fashions of the 1930s* (New Haven, 2014)

Mellor, David (ed.), *Cecil Beaton*, exh. cat. (London, 1986)

Murphy, Sophia, *The Duchess of Devonshire's Ball* (London, 1984)

Nathan, Archie, *Costumes by Nathan* (London, 1960)

Riello, Giorgio, and McNeil, Peter (eds), *Shoes: A History from Sandals to Sneakers* (Oxford and New York, 2006)

Ross, Geoffrey Aquilina, *The Day of the Peacock: Style for Men 1963–1973* (London, 2011)

Ross, Josephine (ed.), *Beaton in Vogue* (London, 2012 [first published 1986])

Sherwood, James, *Savile Row: The Master Tailors of British Bespoke* (London, 2010)

Souhami, Diana, *Greta & Cecil* (London, 1994)

Strong, Roy C., *Roy Strong: Self-Portrait as a Young Man* (Oxford, 2013)

Sykes, Christopher Simon, *Hockney: The Biography, Volume 1, 1937–1975* (London, 2011)

Taylor, D. J., *Bright Young People: The Rise and Fall of a Generation, 1918–1940* (London, 2007)

Torregrossa, Richard, *Cary Grant: A Celebration of Style* (London, 2006)

Vickers, Hugo, *Cecil Beaton: The Authorised Biography*, 6th edn (London, 2002)
(ed.), *Cecil Beaton: Portraits & Profiles* (London, 2014)

Waugh, Evelyn, *Decline and Fall* (London, 1928)

Weight, Richard, *Mod!: A Very British Style* (London, 2013)

Zweig, Stefan, *The World of Yesterday*, tr. Anthea Bell (London, 2009)

ACKNOWLEDGMENTS

Limited space prevents me from mentioning all whom I should, but it is appropriate that I single out Trudi Ballard, William Banks-Blaney, Kate Bassett, John Burrough, Poppy Charles, Martin Crawfood, Richard Cuerden, Giles Deacon, Kate Dooley, Catherine Dunning, Barbara Elsmore, Emma Findley, John Hancock, Rachel Hassall, Colin Heywood, Kenny Ho, Kate Irvin, Lindsay Jamieson, Joanna Ling, John Hunter Lobb, Elizabeth Murphy, Will Newton, Michael Powis, Jayne Prigent, Jason Regent, Giles Reynolds, Anda Rowland, Kathryn Sargent, Sue Simpson, Sir John Smiley, Fiona Smith, Nicholas Smith, John Michael Sullivan, Anna Thomasson and Erica Wolfe-Murray. Special and particular thanks are due to Roger Barnard and Andrew Ginger, who facilitated my research by asking me to contribute to their 'Cecil Beaton At Home' exhibitions in Salisbury and London and to Harold Koda and Jessica Glasscock for their special dispensation to reproduce images from The Metropolitan Museum of Art, New York. Cecil Beaton's former tailor Melvin Stroud; vice-chairman of Henry Poole & Co., Philip Parker; and Cecil Beaton's official biographer Hugo Vickers fielded many questions and they rarely failed to come up with answers. At Thames & Hudson my task has been aided by Maria Ranauro, Faye Robson, my editor Adélia Sabatini, and Jamie Camplin, to whom I remain grateful for commissioning this project.

PICTURE CREDITS

a = above, b = below, l = left, r = right, c = centre

2 © The Cecil Beaton Studio Archive at Sotheby's; 6-7 © Peter Schlesinger; 11 © Condé Nast Archive/Corbis; 12 © National Portrait Gallery, London; 17 AP Photo/Press Association Images; 21, 22 © The Cecil Beaton Studio Archive at Sotheby's; 24l National Portrait Gallery, London. © Estate of Curtis Moffat; 24r © National Portrait Gallery, London; 27 © The Cecil Beaton Studio Archive at Sotheby's; 29 © Bettmann/Corbis; 30, 31 National Portrait Gallery, London. © Estate of Curtis Moffat; 32, 33, 35l, 35r © The Cecil Beaton Studio Archive at Sotheby's; 37 © Condé Nast Archive/Corbis; 39 © Hulton-Deutsch Collection/Corbis; 40-41 Photo Hulton Archive/Getty Images; 43 Photo Gordon Anthony/Getty Images; 44 Victoria & Albert Museum, London; 45 Photo Gordon Anthony/Getty Images; 47 Photo Sasha/Getty Images; 48 © Bettmann/Corbis; 49l, 49r The Costume Institute, The Metropolitan Museum of Art, New York/Art Resource/Scala, Florence; 50 © National Portrait Gallery, London; 51, 53 Victoria & Albert Museum, London; 54 © The Cecil Beaton Studio Archive at Sotheby's; 55 Photo Sasha/Getty Images; 56 National Portrait Gallery, London; 58 Courtesy Anderson & Sheppard, London; 60-61, 63 Photo Sasha/Getty Images; 64 Victoria & Albert Museum, London; 67 National Portrait Gallery, London. © Estate of George Platt Lynes; 69 Photo Warner Brothers/Getty Images; 70a Photo Hulton Archive/Getty Images; 70b © Corbis; 74-75 © The Cecil Beaton Studio Archive at Sotheby's; 76l The Costume Institute, The Metropolitan Museum of Art, New York/Art Resource/Scala, Florence; 76r Courtesy Huntsman, London; 80-81 Photo David Cairns/Daily Express/Hulton Archive/Getty Images; 84-85 © Peter Schlesinger; 88 Getty Images/Bentley Archive/Popperfoto; 89 Victoria & Albert Museum, London; 91 Photo Bob Thomas/Getty Images; 92 Photo Manchester Daily Express/SSPL/Getty Images; 95l Courtesy Shephard Bros. Tailors; 95c, 95r The Costume Institute, The Metropolitan Museum of Art, New York/Art Resource/Scala, Florence; 96 Photo Sir John Smiley; 98 Courtesy John Lobb; 99 Victoria & Albert Museum, London; 100-101 © Norman Parkinson Ltd/Courtesy Norman Parkinson Archive; 103 © The Cecil Beaton Studio Archive at Sotheby's; 105 Photo Paul Popper/Popperfoto/Getty Images; 106-107 Photo Dmitri Kessel/The LIFE Picture Collection/Getty Images; 109 TopFoto; 110 Photo The LIFE Picture Collection/Getty Images; 111 Photo Bert Morgan/Getty Images; 112 © Condé Nast Archive/Corbis; 114 © Illustrated London News Ltd/Mary Evans; 117 © The Cecil Beaton Studio Archive at Sotheby's; 119 Victoria & Albert Museum, London; 123 Sotheby's Picture Library; 125 Photo Peter Mitchell, Camera Press, London; 126 © Norman Parkinson Ltd/Courtesy Norman Parkinson Archive; 129 Photo Arnold Newman/Getty Images; 135 © The Cecil Beaton Studio Archive at Sotheby's; 144 AP Photo/Press Association Images

INDEX

Image references are indicated in bold

Beaton in relaxed attire with his long-serving
secretary, Eileen Hose, outside the winter
garden at Reddish House, Wiltshire, 1960s.